# 99
# WAYS
# TO COOK
# PASTA

# 99
# WAYS
# TO COOK
# PASTA

## Flora and Robert Alda

### With a Preface by
### Alan Alda

Macmillan Publishing Co., Inc.
New York

Collier Macmillan Publishers
London

Macmillan Publishing Co., Inc.
866 Third Avenue, New York, N.Y. 10022
Collier Macmillan Canada, Ltd.

Library of Congress Cataloging in Publication Data
Alda, Flora.
    99 ways to cook pasta.

    Includes index.
    1.  Cookery (Macaroni)   I.   Alda, Robert, joint
author.   II.   Title.
TX809.M17A38        641.8′22        80-11360
ISBN 0-02-500740-8

Book designed by Constance T. Doyle

Illustrations by Sidonie Coryn

First Printing 1980

Printed in the United States of America

# CONTENTS

There are so many people we wish to thank that it would sound like a collection of speeches from the Oscar, Emmy, and Tony award shows all rolled into one. Nevertheless, we must thank them and we want to start where it all began, with our mothers, whose untiring efforts to teach us as we grew remained with us. How fortunate for us that they also loved cooking as we do. And we've been blessed to know that this same enthusiasm for cooking has been passed on to Alan and Antony.

We wish to thank the many restaurant owners who gave us a helping hand with their recipes to add to our collection. Our many friends on both sides of the Atlantic, who so often graced our table, tasting and testing with us. Alan and Arlene for their contributions to this book, and certainly our patient editor Toni Lopopolo for guiding us along the way.

To all our friends, we hope this book helps to bring new friends into your lives, as it did for us.

# Preface

I remember a big steaming pot of red sauce and my father, lean and young, looking into it with quiet excitement, neatly flipping in hunks of meat. Sausages, breasts of chicken, meatballs lightly browned, urged along with garlic, all swam together and mixed their juices under his careful hand.

A thick red river of tomato sauce ran through my childhood and I dove in and splashed around every Sunday. I lived on the banks of a stream that oozed with flavor and was flecked with oregano and basil; bay leaves wafted through it and there were little unexpected bursts of anise and pepper that lightly touched me as I moved among them. To this day I can sit with a spoon and eat a bowl of tomato sauce as if it were soup.

And then there was the pasta. The tubes of every size and cut, the shells, the twirls, the bow ties, the long, long strands you wound around your fork and sank your teeth into to a depth of several hundred yards.

My father was the captain of this river of sauce and the ships of pasta that sailed in it. He cooked as he does most things— with great energy. And he's always loved to spread the word. When he hosted his own daily radio show in New York he filled the air with recipes and cooking talk, even though it was not intended to be a show about food. He loved food so much that just his listing the ingredients made an entertaining program. His enthusiasm was infectious.

Years after that radio program I was in a small Italian grocery store in New Jersey and saw a cheese pie that had been made as a specialty for Easter. It was so rich it was being sold by the slice, but I bought the whole thing. Although the pie was only eight inches across, it seemed to weigh about thirty or forty pounds— and it was wonderful. We ate slab after slab of it. The next day I went back to the store and praised the woman who had made it. I had never tasted a pie like that. I wanted to know what it was called, what was in it. She looked surprised.

"You don't know that recipe?" she asked me. "Your father

gave me that recipe over the radio ten years ago. I've been making it and selling it ever since." I cherish that moment. Across a distance of time and space, ten years later and through the help of a woman neither of us knew in New Jersey, I had been treated to an Easter pie by my father. It was one of the ways, peculiar to a show business family, of staying close while being on the road.

Show business takes you many places, and twenty-five years ago it took my father to Italy for a few weeks. He did a play which led to a film which led to another play and more films, and he stayed in Italy for more than fifteen years. In the course of that time, he relearned Italian—properly this time—and fell in love with and married Flora Marino who had been a film actress. Together, they toured Italy from heel to bootstrap and, if I know my father, ate themselves silly.

I stayed with them in their apartment in Monti Parioli when my father and I did a play together in Rome. Flora lavished me with pasta during that stay, knowing that I chronically suffer from a serious pasta deficiency. I must have those happy noodles slapping against my insides or I begin to look wan and lifeless.

I remember plates of ziti, of Mostaccioli alla Carbonara, of shells with ricotta cheese nesting in their curves and crannies ready to burst with flavor at your slightest chomp.

The true pasta person remembers specific dishes for many years and continues not only to see them but smell and taste them long after what was said and done on those occasions has been forgotten.

I still see a steaming dish of gleaming white rigatoni, topped with a pale red sauce of fresh tomatoes, being carried to the table by my grandmother when I was six years old. Memories like that have a way of lingering.

This is a book of memories for you to create for yourself and for the people around you. Flora and my father have put down recipes not just for dishes of pasta, but, if you're alive at all, for moments in your life.

They love food and they love people. And they love bringing them together.

Join them in these pages, and be included in their embrace.

—Alan Alda

# Introduction

Hello, I'm Flora Alda. I'm pleased that you chose our book from among so many others and I sincerely want to thank you for inviting us into your kitchen. We hope to impart a lot of useful information to you about the making and cooking of pasta. Also some diet "secrets," as well as some entertaining anecdotes.

Hi, I'm Robert Alda. You may have seen me in a variety of roles on the stage or television and motion pictures. But this is the first time I've been an author and chef. I know we'll have a good time and some fun together because I'm really enjoying this new role.

Now, you might ask, what are we doing with a cookbook? Okay, here's the who, the what, the where, the when, and the why (not necessarily in that order). I knew I had an extremely busy season coming up, so one day I casually mentioned to Flora that maybe she should write a cookbook while I was working. "Think of all the wonderful dinner parties you've given in New York, Hollywood, and Rome. Remember how much our guests enjoyed your dinners, particularly your pasta dishes?" Her reply was, "We'll see." I could see she wasn't convinced.

Then one day, several months later, we met our editor and told her the idea about the book. She suggested it would be even better if it were a joint project. That convinced Flora. She knew it would be exciting for the two of us to be working together on something creative. That's how *99 Ways to Cook Pasta* was born.

Everyone loves pasta but most people think it's fattening. Let us tell you at the outset that contrary to popular belief, pasta is not fattening . . . providing you know how and when to eat it. In fact, did you know there are pasta diets? You can actually lose weight eating pasta! There are many little "secrets" we've learned over the years and we're glad to have this opportunity to pass them on to you.

For those of you trying to lose weight and still curb your craving for pasta, try to have your pasta early in the day, preferably for lunch. This will give you more time to digest and more time to burn up calories. As often as possible, use the pasta and vegetable recipes or have your pasta with the lighter herb sauces. Avoid the mixing of pasta with proteins; in other words, the dissociated diet. Having pasta at one meal and proteins at another, makes a "dissociated diet." Friends of ours, famous Italian actresses Anna Magnani and Tina Lattanzi, lost twenty pounds doing this. They ate only pasta and salad for lunch and fish or poultry (with a salad) for dinner. You'll be amazed at how well this works. Roberto tried it one time to get in shape for a play, and he lost twelve pounds.

Then there is the quantity of pasta that should be eaten. It is so easy to overeat when you are enjoying the delights of pasta, but one should try to keep the portion down to 3 or 4 ounces per meal. When dining out, learn to discipline yourself to half an order of pasta. (Split an order with your dinner partner.) Besides trying to keep your weight down, some of you may be watching your cholesterol. In all of our recipes, you may substitute cholesterol-free oils (safflower, sesame, or soy) for the olive. And you may use margarine in place of butter. We can honestly tell you that the difference in the taste is hardly noticeable (but no other substitutes unless specified).

Let us also point out how healthy these pasta dishes can be. Have you ever noticed the skin texture of an Italian *contadina* (a farm girl)? In the old days, we never really knew why their skin was so beautiful and healthy looking. We thought it was all the sunshine and fresh air they got. And it was, but they also ate the simplest things from the earth. Pasta, which is made from wheat, was one of the main staples of a farmer's dinner table. Wheat, tomatoes (for the sauce), vegetables, and herbs are all fine gifts from mother earth. And the oils used were always pure olive oil. We strongly urge that you always use the best products available when cooking pasta. Your recipes will not only turn out delicious but will also be healthful. Just remember, pasta is the food of the eighties (maybe the nineties, too). It's good for your diet and it's great for your budget because it can be served alone or with just about any vegetable. Pasta goes well as a side dish with many leftovers and we've even included a recipe for fried pasta, which means you never have to throw away any leftover pasta.

We've given you some original recipes, some handed down from our families, and some from famous restaurants on both sides of the Atlantic. We sincerely hope this will be a helpful guide especially for the beginner, and if you go into the kitchen with love, good will, and patience in testing and trying, perhaps this book will be a short cut for a great many of you. And by the way, if two of you go into the kitchen together, husband and wife or boyfriend and girl friend, it's a marvelous way to spend more time together and create a joint accomplishment you both can be proud of.

Now that we've met you, you may want to introduce us to your friends.

Good luck, and enjoy.

Sincerely,

Robert

Flora

# 99
# WAYS
# TO COOK
# PASTA

---

## A
## Feast
## in 6
## Acts

# PROLOGUE 1

# THE
# PASTA

Welcome to the wonderful world of pasta. In these days of instant foods, many people not only want their pasta prepackaged, but some folks even look for it already cooked and frozen—"just heat and eat" is the motto. I suppose the reason for that is the kind of pace we're living in these days, but that doesn't necessarily mean we should deprive ourselves of the tasty treats and nutritious foods that mamma or grandma used to make. It really doesn't take that much time and it's certainly worth the effort.

Mind you, there is nothing wrong with the commercial pastas. Especially if you are close to a specialty shop where you can find several imported as well as domestic brands. And these days, in addition to the semolina and durum flours that are being used in good pasta, there are several new brands for the diet conscious. The green noodles, which are made with spinach, can be found in abundance. There is a spaghetti made with artichoke flour and also one made with whole wheat flour or a combination of whole wheat and soya flour. All of these contain more proteins and vitamins and less starch. Any pasta lover can easily develop a taste for all of them.

Ah, but the homemade pasta! Better known as *pasta all' uovo*. We are sure you know how delicious lasagne, manicotti, and ravioli are. Not to mention tortellini or agnelotti! What in the world tastes better than a dish of homemade fettuccine, whether it's served with white or red sauce? You're right! Two dishes of fettuccine.

Whether it's in the supermarket, a specialty store, or your pasta machine, pasta comes in various shapes, sizes, and

3

thicknesses. In many of the recipes we give, you can use any of several different kinds of pasta. Just be sure to adjust cooking time of the pasta.

Today, with the new pasta machines flooding the market from coast to coast, homemade pasta is showing up at the dinner table much more frequently. Mainly because it's becoming increasingly easier and faster to make. By now we probably have your taste buds thoroughly provoked and your gastric juices flowing enough to make you want to attempt an order of *pasta all'uovo*, so here goes. Let's start at the beginning.

# Making Pasta All'Uovo

## Five Scenes

### SCENE ONE: Buying the Fresh Dough

There are many specialty shops around the country today, particularly in the large cities, where one can purchase fresh pasta dough. It even comes rolled and packaged, ready for you to cut to the size and shape you want. For people on the run, some of these shops sell the *pasta all'uovo* already cut in your favorite size and shape, like fettuccine, lasagne, ravioli, etc.; all you have to do is cook it and serve with your favorite sauce. So much for the person who is short on time.

### SCENE TWO: Mix and Roll by Hand

For those hearty souls who like to start from scratch, here are the simple steps to follow. It takes longer to tell you how to make it than to actually do it. The most important thing to remember is patience. The first few times you try to make fresh pasta, it may seem to come out differently each time. So many factors enter into the making of pasta, none the least of which is how well the eggs and flour wish to blend together, that it will take a while for everything to fall into place. You will see an improvement each time you make a batch of pasta until one day, you will feel like a champion and begin teaching others.

Besides the ingredients, you will need: a clean flat working surface (Formica, marble, or wood) about 18 by 24 inches or about 2 feet square, a fork, a rolling pin, a sharp knife, and a cookie sheet or a large piece of cloth (a large cotton dishtowel or folded tablecloth will do).

| | |
|---|---|
| 3½ **cups flour** | ½ **teaspoon salt** |
| 4 **eggs (room temperature)** | 2 **tsp. olive oil** |
| | 1 **Tbs. warm water** |

Place the flour in a mound on your working surface and make a hollow crater in the center. Break the eggs into the crater, add the salt and oil and lightly beat the eggs with a fork. Beating the eggs will cause them to absorb some of the flour. Continue beating and, with your free hand, work some more of the flour from the edge of the crater into the egg mixture. The mixture will begin to thicken. When the mixture is too thick to use the fork, flour your hands and with your fingers work the rest of the flour into the mixture. Slowly add some warm water and begin kneading the dough. If the mixture is too loose or wet you may have to add a bit more flour; if it is too dry, add a few more drops of water. Keep your hands and your working surface well floured. Knead the dough: use the heels of your hands to roll the dough away from you. Then fold it in half toward you, and press and roll away again. Give the dough a quarter turn. Repeat again and again and again until the dough has lost all its stickiness and has become smooth and manageable. This shouldn't take more than 10 to 15 minutes. You now have a golden yellow ball of dough. Cover the ball with a bowl and let it rest in a cool dry place for about 20 minutes. This makes rolling easier.

Clean your hands and working area, and flour both again. Cut the ball of dough into four pieces and with a well-floured rolling pin roll the dough, one piece at a time, into a flat sheet. Keep

turning the sheet so the dough will have a uniform thickness, preferably about ⅛ of an inch. Pasta should be cut into desired widths
before the dough is set to dry, so when you have a flat sheet of
dough, flour it and fold in half, then in half again. (You should
have a piece of dough that is about a foot long and about 4 inches
wide.) You cut this "roll" crosswise into any desired width from
⅛ of an inch up to ¾ of an inch for your fettuccine, fettuccelle,
fettucce, or lasagnette. (Lasagna or ravioli are described in later
recipes.) This recipe is also good for trenette, taglierini, and
tagliatelle.

After you have cut the pasta into the desired width, gently
unroll it and lay the strips on a floured cookie sheet or on a large
cloth (preferably the latter); set the pasta to dry for a couple of
hours before cooking. The dried pasta can be stored in your freezer
until ready for use and needs no thawing before cooking. This
recipe will make enough pasta for about 6 servings.

## SCENE THREE: Mix by Hand, Roll and Cut by Machine

Do everything as above until you have cut the ball of dough
into four pieces. Now use the machine to roll each piece into flat
sheets. Continue to run these sheets through the rollers until uni-
formly thick, then run them through the machine for desired widths
from ⅛ to ¾ of an inch. Set the pasta to dry for a couple of hours
or store in your freezer until needed.

## SCENE FOUR: Pasta Power by Machine!

This is for those lucky people who have a food processor.
You simply follow the instructions on your food processor for
making pasta dough. All it really takes is placing the ingredients
into the mixing bowl of the processor. Half at a time so as not to
strain the motor. Let the two balls of dough rest for 20 minutes,
covered with a bowl, then proceed as above. Use the machine to
roll the dough out in long sheets the width of the machine. Now use
the cutter to cut the pasta to desired widths and let the pasta dry
for a couple of hours before cooking.

## SCENE FIVE : Automatic Pasta Machine

These new machines do everything but cook and eat the pasta. And if your budget allows, you'll find that the latest ones are marvelous. All you do is place the ingredients in the mixer, attach the desired cutter to the machine, turn on the switch, and in less than half an hour, the pasta is ready. Let the pasta dry and cook as desired. One machine we've seen makes twenty varieties of pasta right from scratch. As we've said, all you have to do is cook it. And that, my friends, takes care of the very busy person.

# PROLOGUE 2
# THE
# SAUCES

In the previous chapter we told you all about pasta, the various ways to make it, and the almost countless sizes and shapes it comes in. You might say, basically it's all the same; flour, salt, water, and sometimes eggs. So what makes one pasta dish so different from another? It's the sauce, my friends! And there are many, many kinds of sauces. Every region of Italy, and there are sixteen of them plus the islands of Sicily and Sardegna, boasts of its own special sauces. We've tasted most of these sauces, admittedly not all of them, and we have found the northern regions use more delicate sauces, using mainly butter in place of oil and less tomato sauce. The southern regions are just the opposite, using more tomato sauce and more oil. But regardless of the region, they are all absolutely delicious.

We have listed half a dozen of our favorite sauces. In some of our recipes, we use two sauces, particularly in some of the lasagne dishes. In other recipes, we have taken the marinara sauce and added other ingredients to it, making a completely new sauce. Starting with these six sauces, we have arranged and rearranged them so that we have been able to come up with 99 different recipes.

# A Sauce for Your Pasta

# Six Scenes

### SCENE ONE: Marinara Sauce

½ cup olive oil
2 cloves garlic, cut in half
1 can (1 lb. 12 oz.) *pomodori pelati con basilico* (plum tomatoes with basil)
1 level tsp. oregano
½ tsp. dried basil (or 6 leaves of fresh basil if available)
salt and freshly milled black pepper to taste
1 Tbs. chopped fresh parsley (Italian parsley if available)
½ cup (4 oz.) dry white wine

We have always found that marinara sauce is best when cooked in a large skillet that has a cover, an 8- or 10-inch pan is perfect. Place the oil in the pan and heat. Add the garlic pieces (pieces add more flavor than a whole clove) to the oil and brown. Meanwhile, place the tomatoes in a blender at the lowest speed for not more than a few seconds—you don't want them puréed. When the garlic is golden brown, turn off the flame and let the pan cool a few minutes. Then add the tomatoes and turn the flame back on. Add the oregano and dried basil. (Fresh basil is added at the last 5 minutes of cooking.) Add the salt and pepper, bring to a boil, and let simmer for 30 minutes with the pan covered. Then add the wine (and fresh basil if you are using it), let simmer another 5 minutes, and turn off the flame. Remove the garlic pieces, and the sauce is ready. Serves 4 to 6.

## SCENE TWO: Sugo di Carne (meat sauce sometimes called Ragù)

½ cup olive oil
3 Tbs. sweet butter
2 cloves garlic, minced
½ yellow onion, finely sliced
1 stalk celery, finely chopped
1 carrot, finely chopped
1 lb. lean ground beef
  pinch of rosemary

1 cup dry red wine
1 can (28 oz.) Italian plum tomatoes (hand diced or chopped in blender)
1 tsp. salt
1 tsp. ground black pepper (or to taste)
1 Tbs. chopped parsley

In a large saucepan, heat the oil and butter until butter melts. Add the garlic, onion, celery, and carrot and simmer until garlic is golden brown. Add the meat, crumbling it with a wooden spoon, add a good pinch of rosemary. Stir well, and add the wine. Stir again, cover and cook over moderate heat about 10 minutes. Add tomatoes, salt, and pepper. Bring to a boil, then lower heat and let simmer, covered, for about an hour.

This sauce is usually used with homemade pasta, but is delicious even with store-bought pasta. This will serve about 1½ pounds of pasta (about 6 portions).

## SCENE THREE: Filetto di Pomodoro

6 Tbs. olive oil
1 med. yellow onion, chopped
2 cloves garlic
2 Tbs. smoked pancetta, diced (bacon rinds)
1 can (35 oz.) Italian plum tomatoes (hand crushed)

½ tsp. salt
½ tsp. coarsely ground black pepper (or to taste)
6 or 8 large fresh basil leaves, minced (or 1 level tsp. dried)

In a large skillet, heat the oil and sauté the onions and garlic until lightly golden. Add the diced pancetta and sauté until it is crisp. Add the tomatoes, salt, pepper, and dried basil and stir well with a wooden spoon. (Fresh basil is added at the last 5 minutes of cooking.) Let simmer for about 20 minutes, stirring often. Makes 3 to 4 cups (about 6 servings of pasta).

## SCENE FOUR: Pesto

2 cups fresh basil leaves
2 cloves garlic, chopped
2 Tbs. pignoli (pine nuts)
4 Tbs. freshly grated parmigiano cheese

4 Tbs. freshly grated pecorino cheese (you may substitute romano)
½ to ¾ cup olive oil

This sauce, though very simply made, is probably one of the tastiest sauces in Italian cooking. It adds an exciting flavor to just about any dish. Try a spoon of it on salad; on eggs, scrambled or hard boiled; in a cup of soup; or simply on a piece of toast. Naturally, it goes extremely well with any kind of long pasta. It comes from the Genoa area and the Genovese truly believe they grow the finest and tastiest basil in the world. They may be right.

Place all the ingredients in a blender, using the low, chopping speed. Stop every few seconds and scrape the sides of the blender down so that everything is evenly mixed and blended to a smooth consistency. The sauce can be stored in a jar in your refrigerator for several weeks. Just be sure that, after it is placed in the jar, you add more oil to cover the top of the sauce. Makes enough for 1 to 1¼ pounds of pasta (serves 4 to 6).

## SCENE FIVE: Bolognese Sauce

4 Tbs. sweet butter
¼ cup olive oil
2 slices prosciutto, diced
½ yellow onion, finely chopped
1 carrot, finely chopped
1 stalk celery, finely chopped
½ lb. lean beef, minced
¼ lb. pork, minced
¼ lb. veal, minced
3 chicken livers, chopped (optional)
pinch of rosemary
pinch of nutmeg

1 tsp. salt
1 tsp. freshly milled black pepper
1 cup dry white wine
2 Tbs. tomato paste
1 can (28 oz.) Italian plum tomatoes (hand diced or chopped in blender)
1 cup chicken broth
6 fresh basil leaves (or ½ tsp. dried basil)
¼ cup heavy cream (optional)

This is a very rich and robust sauce but when blended with homemade fettuccine, it is absolutely unbeatable. You will notice that two items are optional, but in this case you should opt for using them. Try it once at least.

In a large, deep skillet, melt the butter; add the oil and sauté the prosciutto, onion, carrot, and celery until the vegetables begin to turn light golden. Add the beef, pork, and veal (and chicken livers if used). Stir well, add the rosemary, nutmeg, salt, and pepper and cook until meat is browned, crumbling it with a fork as you go. Add the wine, cover and let simmer for 5 minutes. Add tomato paste, stir well, then add the plum tomatoes and dried basil, if used. Stir well, bring to a boil, then lower heat and let simmer for 1½ hours. Stir often, add chicken broth occasionally, when the sauce thickens, until all the broth has been used. A minute or two before removing from heat, add the fresh basil if used. If you use the cream, add it at this point. Stir well. Let stand. Makes 3 to 4 cups, enough for 1 to 1½ pounds of pasta (about 6 servings).

## SCENE SIX : Béchamel

5 Tbs. sweet butter
5 Tbs. flour
1 tsp. salt (or to taste)
white pepper to taste

4 cups warmed milk
pinch of grated nutmeg

This is the sauce that is so often used with fettuccine Alfredo. It is also used in many other dishes or sometimes joined by a tomato sauce for certain lasagne dishes.

Melt the butter in a saucepan over a low heat. Blend in flour, salt, and pepper, being careful not to scorch the flour (it will change color if too hot). Cook gently for a few minutes then gradually add warm milk, stirring constantly with a wooden spoon or wire whisk. Continue the cooking until sauce is thickened and smooth. Add the nutmeg.

Pour the hot sauce into a bowl, and lightly whip it with a wire whisk for a moment or two to give it more body. Allow it to cool for 10 or 15 minutes before serving and it will become firmer.

# ACT ONE:

---

# THE
# MEATLESS
# SCENE

When most people think of having some pasta, they immediately conjure up a dish of spaghetti and meatballs. But "spaghetti and meatballs" is an American invention, or at least an Italo-American invention. There are so many ways to prepare a dish of pasta, you could keep busy for an entire year without repeating yourself. In fact, the household in Italy which serves spaghetti and meatballs is very, very rare. Although pasta is a great staple in Italy, meat was always a luxury. Beef was the scarcest of all meats and most families considered themselves lucky to eat it once a week or on some festive occasion. It's been only the last few decades or so that beef has been readily available, and now Italians can't seem to get enough of it.

The scarcity of meat was the very reason so many mothers and grandmothers concocted the many variations of meatless pasta dishes. There was "meatless" pasta with red sauce, *in bianco* (or white sauce), and with many varieties of cheese, such as ricotta or fontina. It was the cook's duty to make the meals interesting by adding variety to the basic staple of pasta.

Today, these recipes are very useful because a great many people are becoming vegetarians or eliminating red meat from their diets. You will find the next twenty-three recipes very helpful for making meatless meals interesting.

14

This was the first pasta dish I cooked for Roberto after we were married. I must admit I knew practically nothing about cooking, but by trying to recall some of the things I had seen my mother and sister do at home, I came up with this recipe for a simple sauce. Naturally, I have improved on it over the years. I now use it as a basic sauce for other recipes in this book. I always keep a jar of it handy in my refrigerator. You never know when you will need a spoonful or two. Enjoy it.

—Flora

## 1. Spaghetti con Sugo alla Marinara

### (Spaghetti with Marinara Sauce)

1 recipe marinara sauce (see page 9)

1 lb. spaghetti (imported if possible)
3 Tbs. salt
3 Tbs. chopped fresh parsley

Preferably, the pasta should be cooked in a stainless steel pot in plenty of water, 5 to 6 quarts to the pound. Bring the water to a boil, add the salt, and then slowly add the pasta. Stir frequently with a wooden fork and cook until *al dente*. Drain thoroughly and place in a large warmed serving bowl. Generously pour the marinara sauce over the pasta, reserving some for your table for those who enjoy a lot of sauce. Then sprinkle the chopped parsley over the pasta. You will note there is *no cheese* in this recipe. The parsley not only adds flavor but makes the dish more appetizing: the green parsley over the red sauce on the white pasta. Call it coincidence, but you have the colors of the Italian flag.

*Serves 4 to 6.*

When I first met Flora in Rome, I invited her to dinner and she suggested Perilli's restaurant. I ordered one of my favorite dishes, linguini with *aglio e olio*. By the time we finished a delicious antipasto, the linguini *con aglio e olio* arrived. The aroma was magnificent. I couldn't wait to "dig in." I looked all over the table and I couldn't find "it," the cheese. I nudged Flora and said, "This is a beautiful place but the waiter forgot the cheese." She began to laugh so hard I had to stop her and ask what was so funny. She then explained that many pasta dishes are served without cheese, and this certainly was one of them. Living in America, I had automatically picked up several of the wrong habits one acquires when dining in Italian-American restaurants, namely, too much sauce or too much cheese where not required or overcooked pasta. Most restaurant owners in this country know better, but they say it's what the customers want. That's why we deliberately left the cheese out of the recipe. Enjoy.

—Robert

## 2. Linguini con Aglio e Olio

### (Linguini with Garlic and Oil)

¾ cup olive oil
3 cloves garlic, finely sliced
1 small dried red chili pepper, broken into two pieces
1 level tsp. dried oregano
3 Tbs. salt
1 lb. linguini
2 Tbs. chopped fresh parsley

Heat the oil in a 5- to 6-inch skillet over a medium flame. Add the garlic and chili pepper. When the garlic is light golden, add the oregano and turn off the flame. Stir it a bit and your sauce is done.

Bring 5 to 6 quarts water to a boil, then add the salt and the linguini. Stir quite often and don't stray too far from the stove. The linguini must be cooked until *al dente*, about 8 to 9 minutes. Drain the pasta thoroughly and place it in a large serving bowl. (Warm the bowl ahead of time if you can. This is simple. Just place it in your oven at 200 degrees while the pasta is cooking.) Dress the pasta with the sauce and toss with wooden forks until all the pasta is well coated. Serve the linguini sprinkled generously with parsley in warmed soup bowls.

*Serves 4 to 6.*

## 3.   Ziti con Ricotta

### (Macaroni with Ricotta)

10  oz. ricotta
 4  Tbs. sweet butter
    salt to taste
 ½  tsp. coarsely ground black pepper
 2  or  3   pinches ground nutmeg

 1  lb. ziti
 3  Tbs. salt
 ½  cup freshly grated parmigiano cheese

In a large bowl, mash the ricotta with a fork, then fold in the butter. Add salt, pepper, and nutmeg and mix well.

Cook the ziti in 5 to 6 quarts salted boiling water until *al dente*, of course. Drain, but not too thoroughly, as a little water won't hurt this dish. Add the pasta to the ricotta, tossing well. Sprinkle the parmigiano generously over the pasta. Serve immediately.

*Serves 4 to 6.*

Penne all'Arrabbiata is a typical Roman dish that you can find in just about any restaurant in Rome (penne are also known as mostaccioli in America). Some make it a bit more *arrabbiata* (angrier) than others, some may make the sauce thicker, but basically it is the same. The penne are not "angry," but the sauce is a bit hot-tempered. We found, after many experiments, that this is the right *misura* ("measure") for us and our friends. But a word of caution. We sat down to dinner at a friend's house in Rome, and along came the Penne all'Arrabbiata. It was delicious but so hot it brought tears to people's eyes. The hostess, or her cook, had put too much red chili pepper in the sauce. In fact, one of the guests was late in arriving, and when he came to the table and saw everyone in tears, he thought a tragedy had struck the household! So take it easy with the red chili pepper. It's easy to add more at the table but impossible to remove it from the sauce once you've cooked it. And did you notice? No cheese. It would detract from the flavor.

—Flora and Robert

## 4.  Penne all'Arrabbiata

### (Angry Penne)

½  cup olive oil
2  large cloves garlic, cut in half
1  small dried red chili pepper, broken into small pieces
1  can (1 lb. 12 oz.) *pomodori pelati con basilico* (plum tomatoes with basil)
½  tsp. salt
1  level tsp. dried oregano
6  small pickled green chili peppers, sliced (*peperoncini sotto aceto*)
¾  cup dry white wine
10  small leaves fresh basil (if available), chopped

3 Tbs. salt
1 lb. penne (or mostaccioli)

In an 8-inch skillet, heat the oil over a medium flame and add the garlic and red chili pepper. When the garlic is golden brown, remove from the flame. While the skillet is cooling, place the tomatoes in a blender and process at the lowest speed for just a few seconds. (We don't mind at all if some of the tomatoes remain chunky.) Add the tomatoes, salt, and oregano to the skillet, and raise the flame to medium until the tomatoes come to a boil. (Cover the skillet, of course, or you'll have tomato sauce everywhere.) After it comes to a boil, reduce the flame to low and let simmer for 30 minutes. Then add the green chilis and wine, cover, and let simmer for 5 more minutes. Turn off the flame, remove garlic, and let stand.

To cook the pasta remember, use 5 to 6 quarts boiling water to the pound. Add the salt, then add the penne or mostaccioli. Stir frequently with a wooden spoon and cook until *al dente*. Drain very carefully because, unlike spaghetti or linguini, the penne don't shed the water easily, since they are tubular. If water remains with the pasta, it will thin your sauce. When drained, place in a large warmed serving bowl. Cover with sauce, reserving some for the table. Toss in the bowl till the pasta is well covered with sauce. Sprinkle the chopped fresh basil over the sauce, and you're ready to bring it to the table. Your guests should be seated so that you can serve your penne hot.

*Serves 4 to 6.*


**W**e discovered this recipe in Torino (Turin), in northern Italy. It was opening night for Roberto in a new musical comedy, *La Padrona di Raggio di Luna*. Roberto has had many opening nights, but this was the first show in which he would speak and sing entirely in Italian! In those days Roberto's Italian was pretty bad, and it was my duty to teach him correct Italian. After only six weeks of rehearsals, here we were at opening night. I sat in the third row center, half scared to death for fear my husband would make some terrible mistakes in the dialogue or lyrics. But I needn't have worried. Roberto performed beautifully, his Italian was perfect, and the show was a hit! After the show we were both famished from all the tension and excitement. Italian shows break very late, and at 1:00 A.M. only one restaurant was still open. We hurried there and found that all they had left was something that had been baked earlier but was easy to reheat. You guessed it, it was Rigatoni ai Tre Formaggi. It was so delicious and we were so hungry that we each ate three portions! By the way, the show ran for a full year in Italy and broke box office records in every city it played. I'm sure this recipe will be as much of a hit for you as the show was for us.

Incidentally, you may notice that the recipe actually has four cheeses. However, since the parmigiano is mainly sprinkled *over* the pasta, it is not counted as one of the cheeses. Buon appetito!

—Flora

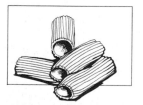

## 5.    Rigatoni ai Tre Formaggi

### (Rigatoni with Three Cheeses)

    3   Tbs. salt
    1   lb. rigatoni

3½   Tbs. sweet butter
    ½   cup shredded Swiss cheese
    ½   cup shredded fontina cheese
    ½   cup shredded mozzarella cheese
    1   cup heavy cream
    ½   cup grated parmigiano cheese
    ½   tsp. ground nutmeg

Preheat oven to 375 to 400 degrees.
To 5 to 6 quarts boiling water, add the salt and rigatoni.

Cook till super *al dente* (very firm), because these are going into the oven. Drain and rinse under cold water, then drain again. (The rinsing is really to stop any further self-cooking.)

In a large bowl, mix the butter into the pasta until it is well coated. Add the three cheeses and the cream. Toss well and add half the parmigiano while tossing. Place in a buttered casserole and sprinkle the remaining parmigiano on top. Sprinkle the nutmeg over everything and bake for 15 to 20 minutes. When the top of the pasta has turned golden brown, it is done.

*Serves 4 to 6.*

There have been many legends on the origin of this recipe. The most popular being that it came from the streetwalkers in Trastevere, the oldest part of Rome, across the Tiber. It was a dish they could whip up in a hurry while waiting for the next "customer." Certainly the name is derived from the Italian word for "streetwalker."

But let me tell you my story. When Roberto and I were first courting, I took him to Mario's, a small restaurant which was famous for Spaghetti alla Puttanesca. He enjoyed the dinner so much that we asked the owner for the recipe. While giving it to us, he mentioned it was given to him by one of the local streetwalkers. We had to believe him because in order to get to his place you had to drive through the Passeggiata Archeologica. Not only is it one of the most beautiful streets in the city, where you can still see some of Rome's archeological history, but it is also a street where dozens of streetwalkers are on display nightly. Roberto nicknamed them the Campfire girls because on cold nights they would keep warm in front of small fires while waiting for the next car to stop. We know Mario's is not there anymore, but I guess the streetwalkers are still displaying their wares.

After dinner, I took Roberto to a well-known spot in the Aventino section of Rome, high on one of the city's seven hills. Near the top was a huge wooden door which was an entrance to a villa. If you looked through the keyhole you could see all of Rome. It was an incredible experience. Looking through that keyhole at the entire panorama of the city, I realized why Rome is called the Eternal City.

—Flora

## 6. Spaghetti alla Puttanesca

### (Spaghetti Streetwalker's Style)

 1  recipe marinara sauce (page 9)

 6  black Sicilian olives, pitted
10  green olives, pitted
 1  Tbs. pickled capers
 3  Tbs. olive oil
 1  clove garlic, finely sliced
 1  small dried red chili pepper (or to taste), broken into small pieces
 1  tsp. dried oregano
 ¾  cup dry white wine

 1  lb. spaghetti
 2  Tbs. salt

While the marinara sauce is cooking, chop the black olives, green olives, and capers very finely (small capers can remain whole). In a small skillet, heat the oil over a medium flame and brown the garlic and chili pepper, about one minute. Then add the olives, capers, and oregano. Cook for 5 more minutes. Add the wine, cover, and let simmer for a few minutes. At this point remove the garlic and chili pepper, then add the mixture to the marinara sauce and let simmer for 5 more minutes.

To cook the pasta, bring 5 to 6 quarts water to a boil, then add the salt and the pasta. Cook until *al dente*, stirring often with a wooden fork. Drain thoroughly, then place in a large warmed serving bowl. Add the sauce and toss till well mixed.

*Serves 4 to 6.*

## 7.  Spaghettini Aromatici

### (Spaghettini with Herb Sauce)

**Sauce:**

¼ cup olive oil
1 large yellow onion, chopped
2 cloves garlic, minced
1 can (10 oz.) anchovy fillets
3 bay leaves
½ tsp. dried ground sage
½ tsp. dried rosemary
2 Tbs. chopped fresh parsley
1 lb. fresh plum tomatoes, peeled and diced
  (you may substitute canned tomatoes)
  salt and freshly milled black pepper to taste
½ cup dry white wine

1 lb. spaghettini
3 Tbs. salt
½ cup freshly grated parmigiano cheese

In a medium skillet, heat the oil and sauté the onions and garlic until light golden. Add the anchovies, bay leaves, sage, rosemary, and 1 tablespoon of the parsley. Cook over a low flame for 6 to 7 minutes. Add the tomatoes and the salt and pepper and cook for 30 minutes. Add the wine, cover, and let simmer for 3 minutes. Turn off the flame, remove bay leaves, and let stand.

Cook the pasta until *al dente* in salted boiling water. Drain and place in a large serving bowl. Pour the sauce over the pasta, add the cheese, and toss well. Sprinkle the remaining parsley over the pasta and serve immediately.

*Serves 4 to 6.*

**S**paghettini all'Ultimo Minuto literally means "spaghetti at the last minute." Both the sauce and the pasta can literally be made at the last minute. The recipe was given to us by my sister, Esperia Marino, who is a very inventive cook and very, very fond of pasta in any way, shape, or form. She is always finding an excuse to cook up a dish. Esperia has been a career woman for twenty-five years. She claims that when she comes home from a hard day at the office she is so famished that only a dish of pasta can satisfy her hunger. She takes a quick look in the refrigerator and says, "The olives are getting dry, the *peperoncini* will go bad, the capers won't last." In a flash, the water is on for the pasta, and while waiting for it to boil, she has her skillet going with all the ingredients. I don't know how many times a week she uses this recipe, but it is one of her favorites because it really can be done at the last minute. Therein lies the story of how Spaghettini all'Ultimo Minuto came to be, compliments of Esperia Marino, Roma.

—Flora

## 8.    Spaghettini all'Ultimo Minuto

### (Last-Minute Spaghettini)

½   cup olive oil
2   cloves garlic, very finely sliced
1   oz. anchovy fillets, chopped (optional)
12   large green olives, pitted and diced
1   Tbs. pickled capers, chopped
6   *peperoncini* (small green chili peppers), chopped

3   Tbs. salt
1   lb. spaghettini
1   Tbs. chopped fresh parsley (Italian parsley, if possible)
1   tsp. freshly milled or coarsely ground black pepper (or to taste)

In a medium skillet, heat the oil over a medium flame and add the garlic. As soon as the garlic begins to take on some color, lower the flame and add the anchovies. When the anchovies have melted, add the olives, capers, and green chili peppers. Let simmer for 5 more minutes, then turn off the flame. The sauce is done.

In 5 to 6 quarts boiling salted water, cook your spaghettini until *al dente*. This takes careful watching and stirring with a wooden fork, as the spaghettini cooks faster than regular spaghetti. Drain and place in a warmed serving bowl. Add the sauce and toss. Sprinkle with parsley and black pepper and serve.

*Serves 4 to 6.*

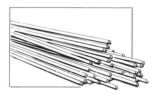

## 9.    Bucatini alla Cipolle

### (Bucatini with Onions)

3  Tbs. olive oil
3  large yellow onions, sliced
   salt to taste

3  Tbs. salt
1  lb. bucatini
6  Tbs. freshly grated parmigiano cheese
3  Tbs. sweet butter
   freshly milled black pepper to taste

In a large skillet, heat the oil. Add the onions, salt, and pepper and sauté very slowly so that the onions do not brown or take on any color but are very well cooked.

Cook the bucatini in 5 to 6 quarts salted boiling water until *al dente*. Drain thoroughly because this pasta is tubular and tends to retain water. Place in a large warmed serving bowl, add the cheese and butter, and mix well. Add the sautéed onions, mix well, then add a generous amount of freshly milled black pepper.

*Serves 4 to 6.*

It's amazing how delicious this simple dish can be. I remember how it saved a terrible family argument one day. It all happened before I met Roberto. My brother, sister, and I were great soccer fans, and as fate would have it, we each rooted for a different team. My brother Ermanno was a big fan of Inter, a squad near Milano. After all, it was the team he rooted for when he went to school in Assisi. My sister, Esperia, was a dyed-in-the-wool Roman fan, and I rooted for the Lazio team. It was difficult to communicate with each other on Sundays, particularly if one or all of our teams had lost. It was worse if one of our teams had beaten one of the others. One particular Sunday all three of our teams had lost, and each by one point. We were all miserable, and to avoid arguments we decided not to meet that night for dinner, as was our custom. The next day we were all at lunch, and some of the gloom remained from the previous day. We were such rabid fans, a loss to our team meant Ermanno's ulcer would kick up, Esperia would get *mal-de-fegato* (pains-in-the-liver), and I would get a tension headache, even before they were advertised on television. In order for us not to get further upset, Esperia suggested a light meal of this delicate pasta and a salad. Fettuccine con Parmigiano e Burro saved the day, with some delicious white wine, of course.

—Flora

## 10. Fettuccine con Parmigiano e Burro

### (Noodles with Cheese and Butter)

1   lb. fettuccine, packaged or homemade (page 5)
3   Tbs. salt
¼   lb. sweet butter
½   cup freshly grated parmigiano cheese
1   tsp. coarsely ground black pepper

Cook the fettuccine in salted boiling water until extra *al dente*, as they will cook a bit more when you toss them in the chafing dish with the butter and cheese. (If you don't have a chafing dish, they can be tossed in a large skillet over a low flame.) Drain the pasta thoroughly.

In a chafing dish or large skillet, melt the butter and add the drained fettuccine. Toss gently with a wooden fork and spoon, adding the freshly grated cheese and the pepper until all the cheese has been added. Serve immediately in warmed soup dishes or bowls.

*Serves 4 to 6.*

This is a dish we shared one Sunday evening in Rome with the Vittorio DeSicas and Shirley and Pat Boone. Pat had done a television show and the four of us went to join DeSica's family at the Stanze dell' Eliseo (Rooms of the Eliseo). It was a kind of theatrical club where theater people would gather for late dinners or between shows on matinee days. The Eliseo is Rome's premiere theater and has been for about half a century.

After a great meal, including Fettuccine alla Panna, only our party remained and the place was rather quiet. DeSica's English was a bit limited in those days but he managed to ask if Pat would do them the honor of singing a song for DeSica's two sons. He explained that the boys were great Pat Boone fans and had just about every record Pat ever made. After that kind of a compliment, Pat couldn't refuse, so he whipped up a fast chorus of "Love Letters in the Sand."

DeSica's family loved it, just as Flora and I did. But as soon as Pat finished, the boys said they'd like to reciprocate by doing something for Pat. Well, they must have rehearsed for days, because suddenly they were doing a full routine of songs, dances, and even some imitations. Of course, it was delightful and we all enjoyed it. In fact, they were so good, Pat had to say, "I was never so glad to open a show. I could never have followed that act!" The boys were only about fourteen or fifteen then, and it must have been their humble beginning. Today, Manuel DeSica is a well-known composer and Christian is a well-established actor in films and television.

—Robert

## 11. Fettuccine alla Panna

### (Noodles with Cream)

1 cup heavy cream
2 Tbs. butter
1 cup freshly grated parmigiano cheese
1 tsp. coarsely ground black pepper
    pinch of ground nutmeg

1 lb. fettuccine, packaged or homemade (page 5)
3 Tbs. salt

Place half the cream and butter in a saucepan or chafing dish over a low flame.

Meanwhile, cook the fettuccine in 5 to 6 quarts boiling salted water until *al dente*. Drain and place pasta in the chafing dish. Tossing gently with a wooden fork and spoon, add the cheese, pepper, and nutmeg, then add the remaining cream and butter. Keep tossing until the noodles are well coated. Serve hot, in warmed soup dishes or bowls.

*Serves 4.*

## 12. Taglierini Verdi al Burro

### (Green Noodles with Butter)

½ lb. frozen or fresh spinach (washed)
    salt to taste
4 cups all-purpose flour
3 eggs

¼ lb. sweet butter, cut into several pieces
6 Tbs. freshly grated parmigiano cheese
1 tsp. coarsely ground black pepper
3 pinches ground nutmeg

Cook the spinach in 3 cups salted boiling water. Remove the spinach, but retain ¼ cup of water. Squeeze the spinach dry and chop very fine.

Place the flour on a wooden workboard. Make a well in the center and crack the eggs into this. Work with a fork until the eggs are well mixed into the flour. Add the spinach and the reserved juice, a bit at a time, working and kneading the mixture into a smooth dough. Make into a large ball, place a bowl over the dough, and let it rest for 30 minutes. Then roll out the dough very thin and cut it into ¼-inch-wide strips. Set out to dry on a cloth or floured cookie sheet for 2 hours. Cook in 7 to 8 quarts boiling salted water until *al dente*, stirring frequently. Drain and place in large serving bowl. Add the butter and mix well. Add the cheese and pepper and toss some more. Sprinkle the nutmeg over the pasta and serve immediately.

*Serves 4 to 6.*

## 13. Cavatelli con Ricotta

### (Narrow Pasta Shells with Ricotta)

1 lb. ricotta
¼ tsp. salt
½ tsp. coarsely ground black pepper (or to taste)

1 lb. cavatelli
3 Tbs. salt
3 pinches ground nutmeg

In a large bowl, crumble the ricotta with a fork, adding the salt and pepper.

Cook the cavatelli in 5 to 6 quarts salted boiling water until *al dente*. Drain, but save ½ cup of the cooking water for the ricotta. Mix the water into the ricotta, then add the pasta in the bowl. Mix well, sprinkle with nutmeg, and serve in warmed soup bowls.

*Serves 4 to 6.*

## 14. Capellini Verdi

### (Capellini with Green Sauce)

Sauce:

- 1 cup fresh basil
- 1 cup fresh parsley
- ½ tsp. dried rosemary
- 2 cloves garlic, sliced
- ¼ lb. freshly grated parmigiano cheese
- ½ cup brandy
- 3 Tbs. olive oil
  salt to taste
  coarsely ground black pepper to taste

- 1½ lb. capellini
- 4 Tbs. salt
  freshly grated parmigiano cheese to taste

Place all the sauce ingredients into a blender and process until everything is well mixed into a thin paste.

Cook the pasta in 8 to 9 quarts salted boiling water, but watch it closely. Capellini are extra-thin and will cook very quickly. Cook until *al dente*, drain, and place in a large warmed serving bowl. Add the green sauce immediately, or the pasta may stick together. Toss gently until the pasta is thoroughly covered with the sauce. Serve immediately. Serve extra freshly grated cheese at the table for those who desire it and keep the pepper mill handy.

*Serves 6.*

## 15. Pappardelle con Noci

### (Wide Noodles with Nuts)

*Pappardelle are wide noodles and are usually homemade. This dish is sometimes called Pappardelle di San Guiseppe because it is traditionally served on the Feast of St. Joseph, March 19.*

|       |                                            |
| ----- | ------------------------------------------ |
| 3     | Tbs. olive oil                             |
| 1½    | cups fine unseasoned bread crumbs          |
| 1     | cup chopped walnuts                        |
| 1     | cup pine nuts (pignolias)                  |
| 1     | lb. pappardelle (page 5)                   |
| 3     | Tbs. salt                                  |
| 4     | Tbs. butter                                |
| 3     | pinches ground nutmeg                      |
| ¼     | cup freshly grated parmigiano cheese (optional) |

In a medium skillet, heat 2 tablespoons of the oil over a very low flame. Add the bread crumbs and sauté until browned, stirring almost constantly. Remove from the flame. In another skillet, heat the remaining oil and sauté the nuts until lightly browned, stirring to avoid burning. Remove from the flame.

Cook the pasta in 5 to 6 quarts salted boiling water until *al dente*. Drain well, then place in a large serving bowl, add the butter, and toss well with a wooden fork and spoon. Add the toasted nuts and bread crumbs and mix everything together well. Sprinkle the nutmeg over the pasta, add the cheese if desired, and serve immediately in warmed soup bowls.

*Serves 4 to 6.*

## 16. Spaghettini alla Carrettiera

### (Spaghettini Cart Driver's Style)

*You will note that this sauce is not cooked but is, rather, a marinated sauce. It is predominant in Sicily and the southern regions of Italy, such as Calabria, where the climate gets very hot. As a convenience, the cart drivers of the early days came up with a recipe that required as little cooking as possible. Simple as it is, it has lasted for hundreds of years.*

6 very ripe fresh tomatoes (not plum type), peeled and diced
8 to 10 large fresh basil leaves (no substitute here), finely chopped
2 cloves garlic, finely chopped
1 tsp. salt
1 level Tbs. freshly ground black pepper
6 Tbs. olive oil

1 lb. spaghettini
3 Tbs. salt

In a large bowl, mix the tomatoes, basil, garlic, salt, pepper, and oil together well, then let stand for at least one hour.

Cook the pasta in 5 to 6 quarts salted boiling water until *al dente*. Drain very thoroughly. Spoon some of the sauce on top of the pasta. Toss well before serving. Serve the remaining sauce at the table.

*Serves 4 to 6.*

## 17. Fettuccine Rosa

### (Noodles with Pink Sauce)

1 lb. fettuccine, packaged or homemade (page 5)
3 Tbs. salt

¼ lb. sweet butter
½ cup freshly grated parmigiano cheese

coarsely ground black pepper to taste
¼ cup heavy cream
4 to 5 Tbs. marinara sauce (page 9)

Cook the fettuccine until *al dente* in 5 to 6 quarts salted boiling water. Drain well.

Place the pasta in a large skillet over a low flame or in a chafing dish. Toss with the butter, some of the cheese, and the pepper. Gently fold the cream into the marinara sauce, mixing it very little, which gives you something like a marbled effect. Add this mixture to the pasta. Toss again with wooden forks until the pasta is pink. Add the remaining cheese, toss again, and serve in warmed soup bowls. By the way, this is good with either white or green fettuccine.

*Serves 4 to 6.*

# 18. Fettuccine con Panna e Uova

## (Noodles with Cream and Eggs)

1 lb. fettuccine, homemade preferred (page 5)
3 Tbs. salt

¼ lb. sweet butter
½ cup freshly grated parmigiano cheese
1 tsp. coarsely ground black pepper (or to taste)
2 egg yolks, beaten with a pinch of salt
½ cup heavy cream, warmed
2 pinches ground nutmeg

Cook the fettuccine in 5 to 6 quarts salted boiling water until very *al dente*. Drain thoroughly.

In a large skillet over a low flame, or a chafing dish, melt the butter, add the pasta, and toss with a wooden fork and spoon. Add the cheese and pepper, a bit at a time, while tossing the pasta until all of it is coated. Blend in the egg yolks, toss some more, add the cream and nutmeg, and toss some more. Serve immediately in warmed soup bowls, sprinkling a dash of pepper over each serving.

*Serves 4 to 6.*

# 19. Vermicelli alla Carrettiera

## (Thin Spaghetti, Cart Driver's Style)

*This is a variation of the cart driver's style pasta. It is used more frequently in central and some northern parts of Italy. The difference between this and the southern style is that there is some cooking connected with this recipe, and some of the ingredients differ as well. But I suppose the cart driver had to consider his use of time as well as the hot climate. That is why both recipes have a minimum of cooking.*

½  cup olive oil
3  cloves garlic
1  large bermuda onion, finely sliced
½  tsp. salt (or to taste)
1  Tbs. chopped fresh parsley
½  tsp. dried oregano
6  Tbs. unseasoned bread crumbs

1  lb. vermicelli
3  Tbs. salt
   coarsely ground black pepper to taste

In a medium skillet, heat the oil, but save 2 tablespoons for the bread crumbs. Sauté the garlic cloves and discard when golden in color. Add the onions, salt, and sauté for a couple of minutes, then add half the parsley and all of the oregano. Let simmer until the onions are light golden.

In another medium skillet, heat the remaining oil, add the bread crumbs, and slowly toast them until golden brown.

Cook the pasta in 5 to 6 quarts salted boiling water. Drain well and place in a large serving bowl. Add the onion sauce and the toasted bread crumbs, tossing gently with a wooden fork and spoon. Sprinkle generously with black pepper and remaining parsley and serve immediately in warmed soup bowls.

*Serves 4 to 6.*

**F**lora and I were doing a hard day's work with my daughter-in-law Arlene. She is well known for her excellent work as a photographer and had been commissioned to do a series of photographs of us, including the cover photo for this book. It may seem like a simple picture, but take our word for it, a lot of preparation and work goes into a photo session, on both sides of the camera. We were just finishing our afternoon's work when Alan came home from the studio. He had just completed his day's work on "M*A*S*H" and was ready for dinner. He took one look at what was spread out before us, which piqued his appetite even more, and said, "I'm starving. Why don't we eat the props?" Well, Flora and I had prepared a little surprise for him. We knew Arlene was going to have a difficult afternoon, so we brought along a jar of pesto, that delicious sauce made from basil. We had enough noodles left over from the picture session, so we cooked up a pot of trenette, added the pesto, and had a feast.

Now, when Alan eats something he likes, he's a hummer. With every succulent mouthful of Trenette con Pesto he would hum, hmmm, hmmm, hmmm, or look up to heaven and roll his eyes. He really enjoyed it and so did Arlene and David Reiss, who assisted her with the shooting. Arlene thought it was the best dish of pasta she had ever eaten. We followed the pasta with an enormous salad, and we had a fitting conclusion to a rewarding afternoon. The pasta and the pictures were perfect.

—Robert

## 20. Trenette al Pesto

### (Narrow Noodles with Pesto)

1 lb. trenette (page 5)
3 Tbs. salt

2 Tbs. sweet butter (optional)
1 recipe pesto (page 11)
    freshly milled black pepper to taste
    freshly grated parmigiano cheese to taste
    (optional)

Cook the pasta in 5 to 6 quarts salted boiling water until *al dente*. Remove with a large wooden fork so that some of the water clings to the pasta and place in a chafing dish (or a large skillet over a low flame). Toss the pasta with the butter until the butter is evenly spread over all the pasta. Add the pesto and toss again. Serve in warmed soup dishes and sprinkle a dash of milled black pepper over each serving, plus additional grated cheese if you desire.

*Serves 4 to 6.*

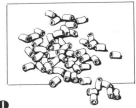

## 21. Ditalini al Basilico

### (Cut Macaroni with Fresh Basil)

*This dish is only good with* fresh *basil, so you'll have to wait until summer unless you live somewhere in the sun belt, as we do, and can grow it all year round.*

  1  **lb. ditalini**
  3  **Tbs. salt**

  3  **cups marinara sauce (page 9)**
      **salt and freshly ground black pepper to taste**
½  **cup loosely packed fresh basil, chopped**
¼  **cup freshly grated parmigiano cheese (optional)**

Cook the ditalini until *al dente* in 5 to 6 quarts salted boiling water. Drain well, then place in a large serving bowl and add 2 cups of the marinara sauce plus the salt and pepper. Toss well with a large wooden spoon. Sprinkle the pasta with the fresh basil (and cheese if desired). Serve immediately, bringing the remaining sauce to the table.

*Serves 4.*

**R**ecently I was in a play with my younger son, Antony, who is developing into quite an actor. We were in St. Petersburg, where we found a marvelous restaurant owned and operated by Raffael and Rita Campanella, who have only recently moved to Florida from Rome. One night Raffael served us a dish of his Gnocchi al Ragù. Antony, who is a gnocchi connoisseur, having sampled them all over Italy as well as in America, said they were the best he had ever tasted. We heartily agreed, and Raffael was so pleased that he gave us the recipe. His secret lies in the fact that of all the recipes we've seen for gnocchi, his is the only one that uses ricotta. It seems to make the gnocchi much lighter. *Buon appetito!* Our thanks to Raffael and Rita.

Campanella's Restaurant
St. Petersburg, Florida

## 22.  Gnocchi al Ragù

### (Potato Dumplings, Ragù Sauce)

- 3  cups all-purpose flour
- 2  lb. potatoes, cooked and mashed
- 2  eggs, beaten
- 2  or  3  pinches ground nutmeg
- ½  lb. ricotta
- 2  Tbs. freshly grated parmigiano cheese
- 3  Tbs. salt

- 1  recipe ragù sauce (page 10)
  freshly grated parmigiano cheese to taste
  extra flour (or cornstarch) for sprinkling
  your hands and workboard

Sprinkle some flour on your hands and on a wooden workboard. Place the mashed potatoes on the board, adding some flour and some of the beaten egg, then mix well. Add some more flour, then the nutmeg, ricotta, and parmigiano cheese, mixing again until all the ingredients are well blended. Keep sprinkling flour on your workboard and hands. Take a palmful of the smooth dough mixture (about the size of a tennis ball), roll it into a ball, then lay it on the board and gently roll it with both hands, flattening it as you roll, so that you end up with a long roll of dough about one inch thick. Set this aside and repeat the procedure until you have about eight or ten long, thin rolls of dough (they will look like uncooked pretzel sticks). Now cut the rolls into 1-inch-long pieces and set the pieces aside to dry for a few hours on a floured cookie sheet or your floured workboard. (Some people like to roll the small cubes down the side of a cheese grater for a different look. This is done by placing the cube of dough on the large part of a cheese grater and pressing with your thumb, down and away. It gives the gnocchi a dimpled effect. They are equally good with or without the dimples.)

Cook the gnocchi in a very large pot of 8 quarts salted boiling water. After they rise to the top of the water, let them gently boil for 2 or 3 more minutes. Remove with a slotted spoon and place in soup bowls, spooning some hot ragù sauce over the top. Some extra parmigiano may be served at the table for those who like to add more cheese. Also keep your pepper mill handy.

*Serves 4 to 6.*

# 23. Spaghetti Fritti

## (Fried Spaghetti)

*This is a very useful recipe for any leftover pasta, especially the long pastas such as spaghetti, linguini, perciatelli, and so on.*

1 lb. spaghetti
3 Tbs. salt

2 cups marinara sauce (page 9)
1 tsp. coarsely ground black pepper
8 fresh basil leaves, chopped
¼ cup freshly grated parmigiano cheese
¾ cup olive oil
½ cup seasoned bread crumbs

Cook the spaghetti in 5 to 6 quarts salted boiling water until very *al dente*. Drain very well, then place in a large serving bowl. Add the marinara sauce, pepper, basil, and cheese. Toss well with wooden forks until well mixed. Divide the pasta in half, placing each half on a separate flat dish.

In a medium skillet, heat 3 tablespoons of the oil, then spread 2 tablespoons of the bread crumbs evenly over the bottom of the skillet. Toast slowly over a very low flame so as not to burn. When the bread crumbs are browned, add the pasta from one of the dishes. Cook slowly for about 5 minutes, or until a crust begins to form on the bottom. Flip the pasta into a flat dish (we usually place the dish over the skillet and simply turn it over, so that the pasta goes from the skillet to the dish). Scrape the bottom of the skillet and put the scrapings on top of the pasta. Now start again. Heat another 3 tablespoons of the oil, sprinkle 2 tablespoons of the bread crumbs over the bottom of the skillet, and when the crumbs are browned, slide the pasta back into the skillet, to cook the other side until a crust forms on the bottom. Flip it out of the skillet. You should now have what looks like a spaghetti pie with a toasted crust on top and bottom. Repeat the process with the second half of the pasta. Serve on flat dishes.

*Serves 4 to 6.*

# ACT TWO:

# PASTA
# WITH
# VEGETABLES

This "act" should have great appeal to everyone who worries about getting the right vitamins. Mothers will love these recipes because they are a simple way to help children develop a taste for vegetables. Everyone knows how difficult it is to get children to eat their vegetables, but by using these pasta and vegetable recipes, they should gobble them up!

Whenever my mamma could, she devised ways to cook pasta and vegetables together, constantly inventing some of the most wonderful and delectable dishes. It was her simple and intelligent way of getting us (my brother and sister and I) to eat our vegetables without any "scenes." I shall be ever grateful to my mother for this because I was able to pass the same idea on to my son, Antony. Let Roberto tell you about his mother's style.

—Flora

Actually, my mother had to work on my father before she started on us children (I, too, had a brother and sister). Papa practically went into a day of mourning when he had to eat vegetables instead of his beloved pasta, and he was not at all enthusiastic the day a pasta and cauliflower dish was on the menu. Mamma tried to prepare him by telling him that "carrots are good for your eyes, spinach contains a lot of iron, onions are good for the kidneys, garlic is good for the blood," etc. So he said, "*Va bene, va bene,* but what is cauliflower good for?" She was stumped, but not for long. She answered, "I don't remember right now but I know it's good for something, so eat it."

We highly recommend starting your children on these dishes at an early age. They are balanced meals containing vitamins, minerals, and carbohydrates. You can be assured they are delicious and beneficial for everyone.

—Robert

**Y**ou may be wondering what D'Asaro means. Let me tell you. It was my mother's maiden name, Nunzia D'Asaro, and that's about as Sicilian as you can get. I was blessed with a wonderful and intelligent mother who studied a great deal about nutrition and it's probably the reason why the three of us, my brother, my sister, and I grew up with such strong, healthy bodies. I'm sorry Roberto never met her because in addition to their mutual love for cooking, they would have enjoyed each other's sense of humor.

She created many of the pasta and vegetable recipes in this book, and her favorite, which eventually became mine, was Spaghetti e Carciofi. She served this very often during the artichoke season. Artichokes contain a great deal of iron. In fact, there is an *aperitivo* in Italy made from the juice of artichokes. It's called Cynar and their slogan is "whoever drinks Cynar, lives to be a hundred." I guess mamma knew the slogan too. I always bless her for making us aware of these great dishes, and I'm sure you will too.

—Flora

## 24. Spaghetti e Carciofi alla D'Asaro

### (Spaghetti and Artichokes)

2 large globe artichokes
½ lemon
½ cup olive oil
4 Tbs. sweet butter
2 cloves garlic, finely sliced

3  **Tbs. salt**
1  **lb. spaghetti**
1  **tsp. coarsely ground pepper (or to taste)**
1  **cup freshly grated parmigiano cheese**

This recipe requires a little patience and a lot of love. First, cut the stem off one of the artichokes and save for later. Now, leaf by leaf, starting at the bottom, you must break each leaf off the stem. However—and this is important—just break off the top part of the leaf, leaving the meaty part attached to the stem. Keep turning your artichoke as you do this until all the leaf tops have been removed. Cut the artichoke in two. You will notice some fuzz or thistle at the core of the artichoke. Carefully remove all of this with the point of your knife. Now slice the two halves very thinly (about ⅛ inch thick). Place in a bowl of water into which you have squeezed the lemon; this should keep the artichoke from discoloring. Repeat this process with the second artichoke and let them both soak in the lemon water.

In a large, 8- or 10-inch, skillet, heat the oil and butter over a medium flame, so that the butter doesn't burn. Add the garlic, sauté for 2 minutes, turn off the flame, and let stand. Place the artichoke slices on a paper towel and dry well. Meanwhile, get those two artichoke stems, peel off the outer covering of the stems, and slice the center parts into small pieces. Place all the artichoke pieces and slices in the skillet and, over a medium-low flame, brown the pieces on both sides.

Now cook the pasta. We have found a marvelous artichoke spaghetti, made of semolina and powdered Jerusalem artichoke, which goes wonderfully well with this recipe. If you can't find it, a good imported spaghettini will do beautifully. Add the salt to 5 to 6 quarts boiling water, then add the pasta. Cook until *al dente*, good and firm. Drain very well, then add to the skillet of sliced artichokes. Mix well with a wooden fork and spoon, adding the pepper and cheese. If the mixture seems a bit dry, you may want to add some more butter. Warm over a medium flame for 2 to 3 minutes and serve right from the skillet in warmed soup bowls.

*Serves 4 to 6.*

**H**ere's another of my mother's vegetable and pasta recipes, and what wonderful memories this one conjures up! Long before I met Roberto, I spent a great deal of my childhood in North Africa, mostly in Tripoli and Benghazi, and some of my most vivid memories were our Friday night dinners in Benghazi. My mother always chose a simple dinner for Friday, and because Friday dinners were always meatless in those days, she usually served one of her vegetable and pasta dinners, like spaghettini with zucchini, a large salad, and some fruit. But that was not the only reason I remember those Friday evenings. It was our regular routine to have an early dinner and then proceed to our terrace which faced the Mediterranean, only 150 yards away. What happened then was one of the most beautiful and spiritual sights I have ever witnessed. Within a few minutes, on the beach in front of us, all of the local North African Jews would gather to wait for the sunset and the beginning of their Sabbath. They were all handsomely dressed in white and the women wore gorgeous white saris. It was their belief that their Messiah would come to them from the sea, and they kneeled and prayed and chanted, facing the sea, until the sun finally set. This happened every Friday night and we tried never to miss the occasion. I truly thank them for it, for not only did I witness some of the most beautiful sunsets in all the world, but I'm sure that I received many spiritual blessings by just being a spectator.

—Flora

## 25. Spaghettini con Zucchine

### (Spaghettini with Zucchini)

- 6 medium zucchini
- 2 cloves garlic, cut in half
- ½ cup olive oil
- 1 level tsp. salt (or to taste)

> **freshly milled or coarsely ground black pepper to taste**

1½ **lb. spaghettini**
4 **Tbs. salt**
¼ **lb. sweet butter**
½ **cup freshly grated parmigiano cheese**

Wash the zucchini, but don't peel, and cut off both ends. This should take away any bitter taste. Slice into thin rounds about ¼ inch thick. In a large skillet (at least 8 inches in diameter), sauté the garlic in the olive oil. Remove the garlic when golden brown and now brown the zucchini in the flavored oil. Place as many slices as possible in one layer only, so that they can be turned over and sautéed until golden brown, about 5 to 6 minutes. This takes a little patience, and you must stand over them so that the zucchini don't burn. Remove them to a large platter and brown another layer of zucchini the same way until you have finished all of them. Sprinkle them with salt and pepper while they are still hot. Save the oil.

Cook the spaghettini in 7 to 8 quarts salted boiling water until *al dente*. Stir often and test frequently; spaghettini cooks quickly. This pasta should be removed with a large wooden fork rather than drained, so that some of the water clings to the pasta. Place the pasta in a large warmed serving bowl, where you have already melted the butter. (Here's a little trick of Flora's. Place the butter in the serving bowl and put it on top of the pot where you are cooking the pasta. It will warm the bowl and also melt the butter. Just be careful the water in the pot doesn't boil over.) Now, over the pasta place your zucchini, add some of the oil you cooked them in, and generously sprinkle some of the cheese over this. Toss gently with a wooden fork and spoon, adding more cheese and black pepper. The zucchini may end up in the bottom of the bowl, so distribute them evenly as you dish out individual portions. We suggest that you make the portions at the table so that they can be hot when served to the guests. Serve in warmed soup bowls.

*Serves 6 to 8.*

**I** first tasted this dish in one of the most inspirational sections of Rome, "I Castelli Romani" (Castles of Rome). Probably the most famous part of the Castelli Romani is Castel Gandolfo, where the Pope has had a summer retreat for many, many years. To be sure, a great many Popes have summered there. The Castelli Romani are made up of dozens of small towns, some on the lake, others on the hillsides, each with its own distinctive characteristics. It is where all Romans spend their weekends at the first sign of warm weather. The area is full of small inns and restaurants, one of which was made famous in the song "Arrivederci Roma," which I have often sung when appearing in night clubs. I believe the line was "si ritrova a pranzo a Squarciarelli, Fettuccine e vino dei Castelli." Squarciarelli's is still there and the food and wine are still excellent. In fact, all the wines of the Castelli are good, the most famous being Frascati.

One Sunday we were invited to dinner to a friend's villa in the Castelli. Usually, I'm a pretty good navigator, but I made the mistake of asking a local cab driver for some directions, just to make sure. Now Romani are very warm by nature and will usually go out of their way to help a stranger. However, in giving directions they will usually indicate the way to the next piazza, "where I could ask someone else." After a while it got confusing even to Flora, though she had lived in Rome most of her life. Well, we finally made it, one hour late, but it was worth the trip. The Spaghetti con Funghi e Piselli was *squisito*, exquisite.

Hope yours turns out the same.

—Robert

## 26. Spaghetti con Funghi e Piselli

### (Spaghetti with Mushrooms and Peas)

½ cup olive oil
1 large clove garlic, finely sliced
6 fresh mushrooms, peeled and thinly sliced
   pinch of salt
2 scallions (including green stems), sliced
2 thin slices prosciutto, diced

1  can (8 oz.) tiny peas
3  oz. dry white wine
1  Tbs. chopped fresh parsley

1  lb. spaghetti
3  Tbs. salt
1  tsp. coarsely ground black pepper (or to taste)
5  to  6  Tbs. freshly grated parmigiano cheese
1  to  2  Tbs. butter (optional)

In a small skillet, place half the oil and all of the garlic. Heat over a medium flame, and as soon as the oil is hot, add the mushrooms, a pinch of salt, and sauté. In another small skillet, place the rest of the oil. Place over a medium flame and add the scallions, prosciutto, and salt. Sauté until the scallions are lightly browned, then add the peas. Sauté together for 5 minutes. At this point pour the contents of both skillets into a large 10-inch skillet, mix the ingredients together well, and add the wine. Let simmer for 5 minutes, or until it almost comes to a boil. Sprinkle the parsley over the ingredients, turn off the flame, cover, and let stand.

Cook the spaghetti in 5 to 6 quarts salted boiling water until *al dente* and drain very well. Add the pasta to the large skillet, toss well with a wooden fork, adding black pepper and cheese. When thoroughly mixed, turn on a medium flame for 2 minutes. If it seems dry, you may add some butter while mixing. Serve hot, right from the skillet into warmed bowls or soup platters.

*Serves 4 to 6.*

I had the opportunity to take Roberto to the city where I was born when he was touring in an Italian musical comedy, *La Padrona di Raggio di Luna* (Moonray's Owner). Roberto won an award for his role, Italy's Nastro di Argento.

In Sicily, we played Siracusa, my hometown. There are many marvelous sights to see in Siracusa, but three of the most famous are the Teatro Greco, L'Orecchio di Dionisio, and the Villa Politi. The Teatro Greco (Greek Theater) is a majestic amphitheater, styled in Greek architecture and built centuries ago. To this day there are performances of many of the classic plays every summer, played by Italy's top artists. The Villa Politi is not only Sicily's most famous hotel, but one of the world's most breathtaking, situated as it is directly on the Mediterranean Sea. In addition to all its beauty, the food is absolutely "out of this world." That's where we tasted Spaghettini alla Siciliana. The next day we visited L'Orecchio di Dionisio (The Ear of Dionysus). In Greek mythology, Dionysus was the god of wine and fertility. Dear friends, you can believe this or not, but shortly after our visit to L'Orecchio di Dionisio, I became pregnant. What's more, my doctor had always told me I could never have children. Was this merely a coincidence? Perhaps, but it was a blessed coincidence indeed.

—Flora

## 27. Spaghettini (or Vermicelli) alla Siciliana

### (Thin Spaghetti with Peppers and Eggplant)

  1 medium eggplant, peeled
    salt
  2 medium bell peppers (yellow or red preferable when available)
  1 can (1 lb. 12 oz.) plum tomatoes
  ¾ cup olive oil
  2 cloves garlic, finely sliced
  ½ tsp. coarsely ground black pepper
 10 fresh basil leaves, finely chopped (or 1 tsp. dried)
  ½ cup black Sicilian olives, pitted and halved
  3 tsp. pickled capers (not salted)
  3 or 4 unsalted anchovy fillets (optional)

½ **cup dry white wine**

1½ **lb. spaghettini or vermicelli (whichever you prefer)**
  4 **Tbs. salt**

Cut the eggplant into slices about ¼ inch thick, sprinkle each with salt, and place on a tilted dish or in a colander to drain off any of the bitter juices. Let stand for about 1 hour, then wipe dry.

Slice the peppers in half and remove the core and seeds.

Put the tomatoes in a blender and crush at a low speed, but not for more than 10 seconds.

In a large skillet, heat half of the oil and sauté the garlic until browned and turn off the flame. Add the crushed tomatoes, a pinch of salt, the black pepper, and the basil and cook gently for 20 minutes.

While the sauce is cooking, cut the peppers and the eggplant into julienne strips (after you have removed the excess water from them). In a medium skillet, heat the other half of the oil. When oil is hot, add the peppers, and after 5 minutes add the eggplant. Stir in the olives and capers. For those who use anchovies, add them now and sauté until they almost melt. (This last procedure should take no more than 15 minutes.) Add the wine and cover. Let simmer for 2 minutes, turn off the flame, and let stand. By this time your tomatoes should be done. Pour the peppers and eggplant mixture into the tomatoes, cover, and let simmer for about 5 minutes.

Cook the pasta in 7 to 8 quarts salted boiling water until *al dente*. Drain thoroughly and dress with the hot sauce. Serve immediately. No cheese please.

*Serves 6 to 8.*

## 28. Spaghetti con Cavolfiori

### (Spaghetti with Cauliflower)

1 medium cauliflower (about 1 to 1¼ lb.)
1 tsp. salt
4 Tbs. sweet butter
¼ cup olive oil
3 cloves garlic, finely sliced
1 small yellow onion, finely chopped
2 Tbs. dry sherry

3 Tbs. salt
1 lb. spaghetti
6 Tbs. freshly grated parmigiano cheese
1 tsp. coarsely ground black pepper (or to taste)
1 Tbs. chopped fresh parsley

Wash and clean the cauliflower, cut into large flowerettes, and discard the thick stems, but save the leaves. Boil in 2 quarts water and teaspoon salt, in a large pot, until about half-cooked. Remove from the pot, but save the water (you will use it later to cook your pasta). In a large skillet, melt the butter, add the oil, then the garlic and onion, and sauté over a low flame until golden brown. Cut the cauliflower into small flowerettes, chop the leaves and add them all to the skillet and cook until it is golden. Add the sherry, cover, and cook for 1 minute more. Turn off the flame.

Combine the reserved cauliflower water with fresh water to make 5 to 6 quarts and bring to a boil, add the salt and pasta. Cook until *al dente*, then drain thoroughly. Add the pasta to the cauliflower sauce and toss gently in the skillet and cook all ingredients together for 2 minutes, tossing gently, adding the cheese and black pepper as you toss. Place all in a large warmed serving bowl, sprinkle with parsley, and serve.

*Serves 6.*

## 29.   Penne con Broccoli

### (Penne, or Mostaccioli, with Broccoli)

1  lb. fresh broccoli, cut into large pieces
3  Tbs. olive oil
2  cloves garlic, finely sliced
½  *peperoncino*, dried red chili pepper
3  Tbs. marinara sauce (page 9)
2  Tbs. dry sherry

1  lb. penne (or mostaccioli)
3  Tbs. salt
½  cup freshly grated parmigiano cheese

Steam the broccoli for about 10 minutes. Drain, reserving the water for later, and cut into smaller pieces (making flowerettes on stems), each about 2 inches long.

In a large skillet, heat the oil and sauté the garlic and chili pepper until the garlic is light brown. Place the broccoli in the skillet. Sauté for 5 or 6 minutes. Add the marinara sauce plus ½ cup of the broccoli cooking water. Bring to a boil, then reduce to a simmer. Add the wine, cover, and continue simmering for 2 more minutes. Turn off the flame and let stand. Discard red chili pepper.

Cook the pasta in 5 to 6 quarts salted boiling water until *al dente*. Remove the pasta with a fork, so that some of the water clings to it. Add the pasta to the skillet and mix well over a low flame for 2 or 3 minutes. (You may also do the last procedure in a chafing dish at the table if you wish.) Add the cheese and reserve some for the table. Serve immediately in soup dishes.

*Serves 4 to 6.*

This recipe is associated with one of the most frustrating evenings of my life. It happened during the early days of my film career in Italy. I was doing a movie for Scalera Films in Rome, *The Five Red Roses*. One afternoon, the publicist came to me and said the studio was throwing a party later that day for an American actor who had just arrived in Rome. He was going to do a film for them. After the party, the studio thought it would be good publicity for me if I went to the Opera and supper with the actor. I asked who the actor was and the publicist replied, "Tyrone Power." I thought of the many times I had enjoyed his performances on the screen. I felt it would be a pleasant evening, so I accepted. We were introduced at the studio party and after the party a limousine picked us up and took us to the Opera. Those of you who know Flora Alda must remember how much I like to talk and exchange ideas with people. I suddenly realized I couldn't speak a word of English and Tyrone couldn't speak a word of Italian. The studio knew this and sent along an interpreter. But speaking through a third party is not the same thing as a tête-á-tête. The Opera was not too difficult, as it afforded little time to talk, but it was terribly frustrating to sit through supper like a tongue-tied dummy. The only thing that saved the evening was this delicate dish of Tagliatelle with truffles and peas. Would anybody believe that an Italian film actress and an American star like Tyrone Power, after spending an entire evening together, would say only four words to each other? I tried "good night" and he tried "Buona Notte." But you never heard such accents!

—Flora

## 30. Tagliatelle con Tartuffi e Piselli

### (Egg Noodles with Truffles and Peas)

6 Tbs. sweet butter
2 scallions (including green stems), finely chopped
3 truffles, finely sliced
½ lb. tiny peas (canned, drained)

1 Tbs. chopped fresh parsley

1½ lb. tagliatelle, packaged egg noodles or
   homemade (page 5)

3 Tbs. salt

½ tsp. freshly milled black pepper

¾ cup freshly grated parmigiano cheese

1½ cups whipped cream (aerosol canned)

In a medium saucepan, melt the butter and add the scallions. Sauté for a couple of minutes. Add the truffles and sauté for 5 more minutes. Add the peas and parsley and let simmer for 2 or 3 minutes. Turn off the flame and let stand.

Cook the tagliatelle in 7 to 8 quarts salted boiling water. Stir frequently with a wooden fork. The homemade kind have to be watched carefully so that they don't stick together. Keep testing until they are tender, but avoid letting them get soft. Drain thoroughly and place in a large warmed serving bowl. Add the sauce, pepper, cheese, and whipped cream as you toss gently with a wooden fork and spoon.

*Serves 6 to 8.*

Situated at the water's edge, Santa Lucia is a very colorful section of the city of Siracusa, Sicily. Besides its very rich and historical background, the city's port and beaches are very picturesque, dotted with local fishermen who are constantly working on their boats and nets. This pasta dish originally came from Siracusa, but you can usually find it in the southern regions of Italy as well as all over Sicily. We seldom were able to find it in northern Italy, but our biggest surprise was to find it in Paris. I was making a picture there with Henry Fonda and Yul Brynner, *Il Serpente* (*The Serpent*). One Sunday afternoon, after visiting the magnificent Cathedral of Notre Dame, we began exploring the many colorful sidestreets off the Champs Elysée. We were completely enraptured by the French atmosphere when, lo and behold, we stumbled upon a small Italian restaurant. To our surprise, the owner (and chef) was Sicilian, and when he found out that Flora was also Sicilian, he insisted on serving his specialty. It's amazing how the camaraderie surfaces when two *paisani* meet, especially in a foreign land. *Ci penso io* (leave it to me) is a line you always hear in Italian restaurants. Naturally we did, and the specialty turned out to be Vermicelli alla Santa Lucia. Sometimes, I think the Italians are as nomadic as the Jews.

—Robert

## 31. Vermicelli alla Santa Lucia

### ("Little Worms," or Very Thin Spaghetti, Santa Lucia)

- 6 Tbs. olive oil
- 2 cloves garlic, cut in half
- 2 cups plum tomatoes, peeled and cut into chunks (canned varieties are usually peeled)
- 4 bell peppers (preferably red or yellow, or both), cut into julienne strips
  salt to taste
- 2 Tbs. freshly grated Pecorino cheese (or Romano cheese)
- ½ cup dry white wine
- 8 fresh basil leaves, chopped (or 1 tsp. dried)

- 1½ lb. vermicelli (or spaghettini)
- 4 Tbs. salt
  freshly grated parmigiano cheese to taste (optional)

In a large skillet, heat the oil and sauté the garlic until golden brown, then discard. Allow the oil to cool a moment, then add the tomatoes and bring to a boil, lower the flame, cover, and let simmer. Add the peppers and salt to the simmering sauce and continue cooking about 20 minutes. Mix in the cheese, wine, and basil, cover and let simmer for 3 more minutes. Turn off the flame and let stand.

Cook the pasta in 7 to 8 quarts salted boiling water, stirring frequently (this pasta must be watched, because it cooks more quickly than others). Drain well and pour into large warmed serving bowl. Cover with sauce and toss gently with a wooden fork and spoon. This may be served with additional cheese at the table. Serve in warmed soup dishes or bowls.

*Serves 6 to 8.*

## 32.   Fettuccelle con Asparagi

### (Narrow Noodles with Asparagus)

20  asparagus tips (the tender part, about 4 inches of the top)
 1  level tsp. salt
¼  lb. sweet butter
 2  pinches ground nutmeg

 1  lb. fettuccelle (page 5) or tagliolini
 3  Tbs. salt
 1  cup freshly grated parmigiano cheese
   coarsely ground black pepper to taste

Cut the asparagus tips in half (about 2 inches long). Place them in a saucepan, cover with water, add one teaspoon salt, and boil until barely cooked, not soft. Drain and let stand. In a large skillet, melt half the butter, add the cooked asparagus and the nutmeg, and sauté slowly until asparagus tips are light gold, then turn off the flame.

Cook the fettuccelle (or tagliolini) in 5 to 6 quarts salted boiling water until *al dente*. Remove the pasta with a fork in order to keep it moist and put it into the skillet with the asparagus. Add the cheese, pepper, and the remaining butter, tossing lightly over a low flame until the butter is completely melted. (You can experiment with this. If it seems to be too dry, a bit more butter or oil may be added just before serving.) Serve directly from the skillet or a chafing dish.

*Serves 4 to 6.*

## 33. Vermicelli alla Sorrento

### (Vermicelli Sorrento Style)

1 can (2 lb. 3 oz.) Italian plum tomatoes
6 Tbs. olive oil
2 cloves garlic, cut in half
½ tsp. dried oregano
6 fresh basil leaves, chopped
1 oz. anchovy fillets
1 stalk celery, chopped
2 Tbs. pickled capers (small ones)
8 black Italian olives, pitted and chopped
1 bell pepper (red or green), chopped
½ cup dry white wine
1 Tbs. chopped fresh parsley

1 lb. vermicelli
3 Tbs. salt

Process the tomatoes in a blender at a low speed for just a few seconds. In a large skillet, heat 3 tablespoons of the oil and brown the garlic. Remove from heat and discard the garlic. Add the tomatoes, oregano, and basil, cover, and let simmer. In another skillet, over medium flame, heat the remaining oil and add the anchovies, celery, capers, olives, and green peppers, cooking until tender. Then gently place all these ingredients in the skillet that contains the tomatoes, stir, and let simmer for 10 minutes. Add the wine and parsley, cover, and let simmer for 5 more minutes.

Cook the vermicelli in 5 to 6 quarts salted boiling water until *al dente.* (They must be carefully watched as they tend to overcook very easily.) Drain thoroughly, then place in a large warmed serving bowl. Add half the sauce and toss well. Serve immediately in warmed soup bowls, bringing the remaining sauce to the table.

*Serves 4 to 6.*

# 34.  Spaghetti con Melanzane

## (Spaghetti with Eggplant)

1  large eggplant (about 1½ lb.)
   salt
½  cup olive oil

1  lb. spaghetti
3  Tbs. salt
4  cups marinara sauce (page 9), heated
1  tsp. coarsely ground black pepper
3  Tbs. freshly grated parmigiano cheese
12  fresh basil leaves, chopped

Peel the eggplant, slice it, and place the slices on a large platter or colander. Sprinkle salt on the slices and place the platter on a slant so that the bitter juices can drain off. Let stand for about 1 hour. Wipe the eggplant slices dry and fry them in a large skillet with the oil until golden brown on both sides. Drain the excess oil on paper towels. Then cut the slices into strips about ½ inch wide and let stand.

Cook the spaghetti in 5 to 6 quarts salted boiling water until *al dente*. Place in a large serving bowl. Add half the marinara sauce, all of the eggplant slices, and the black pepper. Toss well, mixing the eggplant throughout. Add a bit more sauce, reserving some for the table. Sprinkle the cheese generously over the pasta and dot with the basil leaves. Serve immediately, in warmed soup bowls.

*Serves 4 to 6.*

## 35. Spaghettini con Verza

### (Thin Spaghetti with Cabbage)

2 Italian sausages (1 mild, 1 hot)
½ cup olive oil
1 small yellow onion, chopped
2 cloves garlic, minced
   pinch of dried rosemary
1 medium head cabbage, parboiled and chopped
   salt and freshly milled black pepper to taste
½ cup warm water
½ cup dry white wine

1 lb. spaghettini
3 Tbs. salt

Parboil the sausages for a few minutes to remove the excess grease. In a large skillet, heat the oil and sauté the onion and garlic until golden. Remove the sausage skins, crumble the meat, and add to the skillet. Add the rosemary and brown the sausage meat. Add the cabbage and the salt and pepper. Mix well and sauté for 5 minutes. Add the warm water and wine, cover, and let simmer for 15 minutes, or until the cabbage is tender.

Cook the spaghettini in 5 to 6 quarts salted boiling water until *al dente*. Drain and place in a large serving bowl. Pour the cabbage and sausage mixture over the pasta. Mix well and serve immediately in warmed soup bowls.

*Serves 4 to 6.*

## 36. Cavatelli con Caponata

### (Cavatelli, a Small Macaroni, with Caponata)

½ cup olive oil
1 yellow onion, chopped
½ cup chopped hearts of celery
3 bell peppers (green and/or red), cut into
 1-inch squares
2 zucchini, peeled and diced
1 medium eggplant, peeled and diced
 salt and freshly milled black pepper to taste
1 tsp. dried oregano
2 tsp. pickled capers
6 large green olives, pitted and chopped
½ cup marinara sauce (page 9)
½ cup dry white wine
6 to 8 fresh basil leaves (or 1 tsp. dried)

1 lb. cavatelli
3 Tbs. salt

In a large skillet, heat the oil and add the onion, celery, and peppers. Sauté until the peppers take on a little color (when they begin to brown). Add the zucchini and eggplant, salt and pepper, and oregano. Mix well and let simmer until tender. Add the capers, olives, and marinara sauce. Mix well, cover, and let simmer for a few minutes. Add the wine and basil, cover, and let simmer for 3 more minutes. When the caponata is ready, turn off the flame and let stand.

Cook the cavatelli in 5 to 6 quarts salted boiling water until *al dente*. Drain thoroughly, leaving not a drop of water. Add the pasta to the caponata, mix well, and serve directly from the skillet or from a large chafing dish in warmed soup bowls.

*Serves 6 to 8.*

## 37. Spaghettini con Escarole e Fagioli

### (Thin Spaghetti with Escarole and Beans)

  1  head escarole
  1  tsp. salt
  ¼  cup olive oil
  1  clove garlic, cut in half
  ½  dried red chili pepper
  ¼  yellow onion, finely chopped
  2  slices bacon, diced
  ¼  cup marinara sauce (page 9)
  ½  cup dry sherry
  1  can (20 oz.) *canellini* (white pinto beans)

  ½  lb. spaghettini
1½  Tbs. salt

Peel off the leaves from the escarole, wash thoroughly, and cut into pieces. In a 5-quart saucepan, boil about 6 cups salted water and cook the escarole until tender. In a small skillet, heat the oil and sauté the garlic, chili pepper, and onion until light golden. Add the bacon and sauté until crisp. Add marinara sauce and wine, cover, and let simmer for 5 minutes, then discard garlic and chili. Add the beans, with their juices, to the escarole in the saucepan and mix well. Then add the marinara sauce mixture. Mix well, cover, and bring to a boil, then lower the flame and let simmer for a few minutes. Turn off the flame and let stand.

Cook the pasta in 3 quarts salted boiling water until extra *al dente*. Watch it carefully, stirring often, as spaghettini cooks very quickly. Drain well and add the pasta to the escarole. Mix well and cook all together for a few minutes. (Here's where you can add an extra cup of water if it seems too dry.) Let stand for a few minutes before serving. Serve in soup bowls.

*Serves 4 to 6.*

# 38. Vermicelli con Broccoli di Rapa

## (Very Thin Spaghetti with Rapini)

*Broccoli di rapa differs from the broccoli most of us know. It is mostly leaves with tiny unopened flowers and has a slightly bitter taste when cooked. In the western United States it is called rapini. Ask for it under either name. It is not always easy to find, but once you've found it, you are certain to become a big fan because of its distinctive flavor.*

1½  lb. broccoli di rapa
 1  tsp. salt
 6  Tbs. olive oil
 2  cloves garlic
 ½  dried red chili pepper
 2  cups Italian plum tomatoes, peeled and diced
    salt to taste
 ½  tsp. dried basil
 ½  cup dry white wine

 1  lb. vermicelli
 3  Tbs. salt
    freshly grated parmigiano cheese, to taste
    (optional)

Wash the rapini thoroughly, removing any extra-long stems. Steam or boil the leaves in 6 cups salted boiling water until tender. Drain, reserving the cooking water for later.

In a medium skillet, heat the oil and lightly brown the garlic and chili pepper. Add the tomatoes, salt, and basil, mix well, cover, and cook for 10 minutes over medium flame. Add the wine, cover, and let simmer for 5 minutes. Then add the cooked rapini and 1 cup of the rapini cooking water and mix well. Bring to a boil, then turn off the flame and let stand.

Cook the pasta in 5 to 6 quarts salted boiling water, stirring frequently, until *al dente*. Remove the vermicelli with a fork and add to the rapini. Mix together over a medium flame. Serve in soup bowls. If you desire, sprinkle some cheese over each serving.

*Serves 4 to 6.*

## 39.  Linguini con Broccoli e Cavolfiori

### (Linguini with Broccoli and Cauliflower)

6 Tbs. olive oil
½ dried red chili pepper
2 cloves garlic, minced
1 can (1 lb. 12 oz.) Italian plum tomatoes, diced
  salt to taste
1 tsp. dried basil
3 bay leaves
2 cups broccoli flowerettes, partially boiled or steamed
2 cups cauliflower flowerettes, partially boiled or steamed
½ cup dry sherry

1 lb. linguini
3 Tbs. salt
  freshly grated parmigiano cheese to taste (optional)

In a large skillet, heat the oil and sauté the chili pepper and garlic until light golden. Squeeze or crush the tomatoes by hand and add them, along with the salt, basil, and bay leaves, to the skillet. Mix well, cover, and cook for 20 minutes over moderate flame. When the tomatoes are done, add the greens and sherry, cover, and let simmer for 5 minutes. Turn off the flame, remove bay leaves, and let stand.

In 5 to 6 quarts salted boiling water cook the pasta until *al dente*. Drain well and place in a large serving bowl. Pour the sauce over it, toss well, and serve immediately in soup dishes. Some cheese may be sprinkled over each serving if you wish.

*Serves 4 to 6.*

## 40.  Fettuccelle alla Genovese

### (Medium Noodles Genoa Style)

1  Tbs. salt
1  lb. potatoes, boiled, skinned, and cubed
1  package (10 oz.) frozen french-cut beans

1  lb. fettuccelle, preferably homemade (page 5)
3  Tbs. salt
1  recipe for pesto (page 11)
3  Tbs. freshly grated parmigiano cheese
1  tsp. coarsely ground black pepper

To a medium pot of boiling water add the 1 tablespoon salt and cook the cubed potatoes for 6 minutes. Add the green beans, and when the water returns to boiling, cook for 10 more minutes, or until tender, then drain.

Cook the pasta in 5 to 6 quarts salted boiling water until *al dente*. Remove from pot with a fork and place in a large serving bowl. Don't discard the pasta water, as you will use some of it later. Add the potatoes and beans to the pasta, mix well, and add the pesto. If the sauce seems a bit too thick, you can dilute it with some of the water you cooked the pasta in. Add the cheese and black pepper. Toss gently with a wooden fork and spoon until the pasta is well coated with the pesto. Serve in soup bowls.

*Serves 4 to 6.*

# ACT THREE:

# MINESTRE
# Main-meal
# Soups

The more we worked on this book, the more it awakened our "memory buds," to coin a phrase. It seemed to be that way for both Flora and me. She began thinking about all the memorable things we did together and my mind wandered all the way back to my boyhood. She has a marvelous Italian phrase for it: *spremere il mio cervello*, which means "to squeeze my brain" (as in juicing).

We were coming to the "act" on minestra and we began thinking and talking about "pasta and piselli," "pasta and lenticchie," and "pasta and fagioli." Now some people might call these dishes soups, but not the way we had them at home. They are more like a "meatless stew," containing many herbs and spices and some "hidden" vegetables which are practically melted into the *minestra*. They are quite hearty dishes, especially on a cool fall day or a cold winter evening, when some people add hot chili pepper seeds to them. In Italy we call it a dish made *casareccio*, or home style.

You will find *minestra* a very flexible dish, because a small portion may be used as a first dish, or *primo piatto*, as they say in Italy. A large portion can be a meal in itself, especially when it is accompanied by a slice or two of toasted French or Italian bread. A wholesome dish of minestra, a small salad, and a piece of fresh fruit for dessert and you have a complete, nutritious, and economical meal.

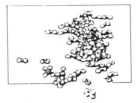

# 41. Farfalline con Fave e Piselli

## ("Small Butterflies" with Peas and Fava Beans)

    3 Tbs. olive oil
    1 Tbs. sweet butter
    4 scallions, finely chopped
    4 thin slices prosciutto, diced
   10 oz. (half of a 20 oz. can) green fava beans,
      drained
      salt to taste
      coarsely ground black pepper to taste (the
      more the better)
    2 Tbs. chopped fresh parsley
    1 cup warm water
    1 chicken bouillon cube
    1 can (8 oz.) tiny peas, drained
   ½ cup dry white wine
   ½ lb. farfalline
  1½ Tbs. salt

In a 3-quart pot, heat the oil and butter and add the scallions and prosciutto. Sauté until browned. Add the fava beans, salt, pepper, parsley, and the cup of warm water. Bring to a boil, add the bouillon cube and the peas, and let simmer for 5 minutes. Add the wine, cover, and let simmer for 5 more minutes. If too much liquid evaporates, add a bit more water. Then turn off the flame and let stand.

Cook the farfalline *al dente* in 2 quarts salted boiling water. Drain the pasta well, then add it to the first pot. Stir well over medium-high flame. When the first bubbles appear, turn off the flame and let stand for a couple of minutes before serving.

*Serves 4 to 6.*

I made about fifteen movies in Italy, but the one in which I had the most fun was *Totó and Peppino al Muro di Berlino* (*Totó and Peppino at the Berlin Wall*). It was a satire on Stanley Kramer's *Nuremburg Trials*. I played a judge and it was the first movie in which I actually spoke my role entirely in Italian. It was not only a joy, but an achievement for me.

It was also a great thrill to be doing a film with two of Italy's great comedians: Totó, who was then considered the Italian Charles Chaplin, and Peppino DeFilippo, who came from a well-known theatrical family. Peppino's sister, Titina, had a great career in the theater and films, and his brother, Eduardo, also well known in the theater and films, was a successful author of theatrical comedies. Both Totó and Peppino were Neopolitans, where my family roots are. Along about noon each day, like all good Neopolitans, they began discussing the kind of pasta we were going to have for lunch. You see, with Neopolitans, a meal is not a meal without pasta. One night, we went to dinner with Peppino, and very proudly he told Flora and me, "You have never tasted Pasta and Fagioli like this in your entire life." He was right, we had never tasted Pasta and Fagioli like it but since then, I must confess, we have often made Pasta and Fagioli con Tre Paste, and we always think of Peppino DeFilippo.

—Robert

## 42.   Pasta e Fagioli con Tre Paste

### (Pasta and Beans with Three Kinds of Pasta)

  1 lb. dried *canellini* (white pinto beans)
  ¼ cup olive oil
  ½ yellow onion, finely chopped
  2 hearts of celery (with tops), finely chopped
  ½ carrot, finely chopped
  3 Tbs. marinara sauce (page 9)
  ½ cup dry white wine
  1 chicken bouillon cube

5 oz. spaghetti, broken into 2-inch pieces
5 oz. fettuccine, broken into 2-inch pieces
5 oz. ditalini
3 Tbs. salt
1 tsp. coarsely ground black pepper

Soak the beans overnight. Rinse and boil in fresh water in a pot about the size of a dutch oven, using enough water to cover the beans by an inch or two. Add 1 tablespoon of the oil to the beans as they cook (it tenderizes them). Cook the beans until *al dente*, about 30 to 45 minutes. In a medium skillet, heat the remaining 2 tablespoons oil, add the onion, celery, and carrot, and sauté for a few minutes. Then add the marinara sauce and wine, cover, and let simmer for a few minutes. Add this *soffrito* to the beans. Also add the bouillon cube. Bring the mixture to a boil, then lower the flame and let simmer for 5 minutes.

The next part requires a little patience. You must cook the three types of pasta in three different pots. Cook each in 1½ quarts boiling water with 1 tablespoon of the salt until very *al dente*. Drain well. Add the pasta, one kind at a time, to the beans. Add pepper and mix well. Let everything simmer together for 5 or 6 minutes. Serve in warmed soup bowls.

*Serves 6 to 8.*

I remember eating Pasta e Piselli for the first time when my maternal grandmother made it. She was a petite woman who had come from Basilicata, in southern Italy. She must have been quite a gal. I only knew her the last fifteen years of her life. I never knew my maternal grandfather because by the time I showed up on this planet, Grandma was on her third husband, a wonderful seaman from Sicily. Everyone in the family loved him and was loved in return. Forgive me for waxing so sentimental, but that's what this book has done to us. Anyway, this dish was a regular

Wednesday night special at our house when I was a kid, and I just had to include it in this book.

Some refer to this as a soup dish, but it is a hearty *primo piatto*. Some also make it drier than others.

—Robert

# 43. Pasta e Piselli

## (Macaroni with Peas)

¼ cup olive oil
2 scallions, finely chopped
2 thin slices prosciutto, diced
1 can (1 lb.) tiny peas
½ tsp. salt (or to taste)
1 tsp. coarsely ground black pepper (or to taste)
2 Tbs. chopped fresh parsley
2 Tbs. dry sherry
¼ cup marinara sauce (page 9)
1 beef bouillon cube
2 cups hot water

1½ Tbs. salt
½ lb. ditalini

In a 3- or 4-quart pot, heat the oil, add the scallions and prosciutto, and sauté over a low flame for 5 minutes. Add the peas, salt and pepper, and parsley and sauté for 3 more minutes. Add the sherry and marinara sauce, mix well, and continue cooking for 2 more minutes. Add the bouillon cube and the hot water. Bring to boil, turn off the flame, cover, and let stand.

In 3 quarts salted boiling water, cook the ditalini until very *al dente*. Drain the pasta and add it to the peas and sauce. Cook together for about 5 more minutes. Serve in warmed soup dishes.

*Serves 6.*

## 44. Ditalini con Fave

### (Ditalini with Fava Beans)

    3  Tbs. olive oil
    1  Tbs. sweet butter
    2  scallions, chopped
    4  thin slices lean baked ham, diced
    1  can (20 oz.) fava beans, drained
       salt and freshly milled black pepper to taste
    2  Tbs. chopped fresh parsley
    1  cup warm water
    1  chicken bouillon cube
    ½  cup dry white wine

 1½  Tbs. salt
    ½  lb. ditalini

In a medium saucepan, heat the oil and butter and add the scallions and ham. Sauté until browned. Add the fava beans, salt and pepper to taste, parsley, and the cup of warm water. Bring to a boil, add the bouillon cube, and let simmer for 5 minutes. Add the wine, cover, and let simmer for 5 more minutes. Don't let the liquid evaporate, or you may have to add more water. Turn off the flame and let stand.

In another pot of 1 quart salted boiling water, cook the ditalini until *al dente*. Drain well, then add the pasta to the first pot placed over a medium high flame. Mix well. When the first bubbles appear, turn off the flame. Let stand for a couple of minutes before serving. Serve in warmed soup plates.

*Serves 4 to 6.*

## 45.  Minestra di Farfalline con Zucchini

### ("Small Butterflies" and Zucchini)

6 medium zucchini
6 Tbs. olive oil
2 carrots, finely chopped
1 yellow onion, finely chopped
    salt and freshly milled pepper to taste
½ tsp. dried oregano
½ tsp. dried basil
3 Tbs. marinara sauce (page 9)
2 chicken bouillon cubes
¾ cup dry white wine
4 cups water
½ cup parmigiano cheese, freshly grated

1 Tbs. salt
2 cups farfalline

Wash the zucchini and partially peel them, leaving some of the green skin on for color. Take a thin slice off from each end, then quarter them lengthwise. Hold the quarters together and cut into ½-inch-long slices.

In a 5-quart saucepan or dutch oven, heat the oil and add the carrots and onion. Sauté until onion is golden. Add the zucchini, salt and pepper, oregano, basil, and marinara sauce. Mix well, then sauté for a few minutes, stirring frequently. Add the bouillon cubes and wine, cover, and let simmer for 5 or 6 minutes. Add the water, bring to a boil, then lower the flame. Stir in 2 tablespoons of the cheese, cover, and let simmer for 15 minutes.

In 2 quarts of salted boiling water, cook the farfalline until *al dente*, drain and add to the other saucepan. Stir well, and let simmer for 5 more minutes. Serve in soup bowls with some of the remaining cheese sprinkled over each serving.

*Serves 4 to 6.*

# 46. Minestra di Lenticchie con Ditalini

## (Thick Lentil and Macaroni Soup)

2 qt. water
1 tsp. salt
½ lb. lentils, soaked overnight
1 stalk celery (with leaves), finely chopped
¼ cup olive oil
½ yellow onion, finely sliced
½ dried red chili pepper (optional)
¼ cup marinara sauce (page 9)
½ cup dry white wine

2 cups ditalini
2 Tbs. salt
salt and freshly milled black pepper to taste

In a medium saucepan of salted water, bring the lentils to a boil. Add the chopped celery and 1 tablespoon of the oil. Cook over a medium flame until tender, about 45 to 50 minutes.

Meanwhile, in a small skillet, heat the remaining oil, add the onion and chili pepper, and sauté until light golden. Add the marinara sauce, mix well, and let simmer for a couple of minutes. Add the wine, cover, and let simmer for 5 more minutes. Turn off the flame and let stand. When the lentils are cooked, add these ingredients to the lentils. Stir well and let simmer for 5 minutes.

In a small pot, cook the ditalini in 3 quarts salted boiling water for about 5 or 6 minutes. Drain the pasta and add it to the lentils. Stir well and let all simmer together for about 5 minutes. Turn off the flame and let stand for a few minutes before serving. Serve in warmed soup bowls.

*Serves 4 to 6.*

## 47.   Spaghetti con Lenticchie e Spinaci

### (Spaghetti with Lentils and Spinach)

1   package (10 oz.) frozen chopped spinach
    (or fresh if you have time)
    pinch of salt
¼   cup olive oil
¼   onion, chopped
1   clove garlic, minced
2   slices bacon, diced
¼   cup marinara sauce (page 9)
½   cup dry sherry
1   can (20 oz.) lentil soup

½   lb. spaghetti, broken into pieces about 1½ to
    2 inches
2   Tbs. salt
    coarsely ground black pepper to taste

In a 3-quart saucepan, place 3 cups of water and the spinach and bring to a boil. Add a pinch of salt. While the spinach is cooking, heat the oil in a small skillet, add the onion and garlic, and sauté till lightly golden. Add the bacon and cook until crisp. Add the marinara sauce, sherry, cover, and let simmer for 5 minutes. When the spinach is cooked, add the skillet ingredients to the saucepan. Mix well and bring to a boil. Add the lentil soup, lower the flame, and cook for 5 minutes. Turn off the flame and let stand.

Cook the broken spaghetti in 3 quarts salted boiling water for 5 or 6 minutes (parcooked). Drain and add to the lentil-spinach mixture. Add pepper. Mix well, bring to a boil, then let simmer for 5 minutes over a low flame. The right consistency is important for a *minestra*—not too soupy, but not too dry either—so if necessary, add a cup of warm water, mixing well. Turn off the flame and let stand for a few minutes before serving to consolidate the flavors. Serve in soup bowls.

*Serves 4 to 6.*

# 48. Lumachine e Fagioli (often called Pasta e Fazul)

## ("Small Snails" and Beans)

*During summers in Rome, this dish is also served cold. With a little olive oil over it, it is delicious.*

½ lb. *canellini* (white pinto beans)
   salt to taste
1 heart of celery, finely chopped
¼ cup olive oil
2 scallions, finely chopped
2 thin slices prosciutto, diced
½ dried red chili pepper
½ cup dry sherry
3 Tbs. marinara sauce (page 9)

2 cups lumachine
2 Tbs. salt

Soak the beans overnight. Rinse and boil, along with the celery, in a 5-quart saucepan with about 6 cups salted water and 1 tablespoon of the oil (this tenderizes the beans). Cook 30 to 45 minutes, or until tender.

In a small skillet, heat the remaining oil. Add the scallions, prosciutto, and chili pepper. Sauté until the prosciutto is crisp (be careful not to burn the scallions). Add the sherry, cover, and let simmer for 5 minutes. Add the marinara sauce, mix well, and bring to a boil, then turn off the flame and let stand. Add the ingredients of the skillet to the beans, mix well, and let simmer together for a few minutes. Remove from the flame and let stand.

Cook the pasta in 5 to 6 quarts salted boiling water for 6 minutes. Drain and add to the beans. Stir well and let simmer together for 3 minutes. Turn off the flame and let stand a couple of minutes before serving. Serve in warmed soup bowls.

*Serves 4 to 6.*

# 49. Maruzzelle con Piselli Secci

### (Small Shells with Split Peas)

6 Tbs. olive oil
½ medium yellow onion, finely sliced
2 scallions, diced
4 thin slices lean prosciutto, diced
½ cup dry sherry
1 Tbs. finely chopped fresh parsley
2 20-oz. cans split pea soup
 salt to taste
1 tsp. coarsely ground black pepper

½ lb. maruzzelle
1½ Tbs. salt

In a 5-quart saucepan, heat the oil and sauté the onion and scallions until golden brown. Add the prosciutto and sauté till well done. Add the sherry and parsley, cover, and let simmer for a few minutes. Add all the contents of the two cans of split pea soup, salt to taste, add the pepper and cook for 5 minutes.

Cook the pasta in 3 quarts salted boiling water until very *al dente*. Drain quickly, but not too well, so that some water is retained in the shells. Add the pasta to the pea soup. Stir well and cook, covered, over a low flame for 2 to 3 minutes. Turn off the flame and let stand a few minutes before serving. Serve in soup bowls, adding a dash of black pepper over each serving.

*Serves 8.*

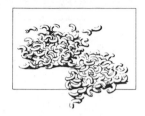

# 50.  Pasta e Ceci

## (Elbow Macaroni with Garbanzo Beans)

¼  cup olive oil
2  scallions, finely chopped
1  can (20 oz.) *ceci* (garbanzo beans)
½  tsp. dried rosemary
   salt to taste
1  tsp. coarsely ground black pepper
¼  cup marinara sauce (page 9)

2  Tbs. salt
½  lb. elbow macaroni
4 to 6 Tbs. olive oil (optional)

In a 5-quart saucepan, heat the oil and sauté the scallions until golden. Add the *ceci*, with their liquid, rosemary, salt, pepper, and marinara sauce. Mix well and cook over medium flame, covered, for 5 minutes.

Cook the pasta in 2 quarts salted boiling water until very *al dente*. Drain quickly, but not too well, so that some of the water remains with the pasta. Add the pasta to the *ceci*, mix well, and cook together for 3 minutes. Turn off the flame and let stand for a couple of minutes before serving. Serve in soup bowls.

In Sicily, approximately 1 tablespoon of olive oil is poured over each serving with a dash of black pepper.

*Serves 4 to 6.*

## 51. Minestrone con Orecchiette

### (Vegetable Soup with "Small Ears")

6 Tbs. olive oil
1 medium yellow onion, chopped
½ cup chopped celery
½ cup diced carrots
1 cup diced peeled potatoes
1 cup diced peeled zucchini
2 qt. water
1 package (10 oz.) frozen chopped spinach
   (or fresh if you prefer)
½ tsp. dried basil
1 Tbs. chopped fresh parsley
   salt and coarsely ground black pepper to taste
½ cup dry white wine
2 chicken bouillon cubes
3 Tbs. marinara sauce (page 9)
3 Tbs. freshly grated parmigiano cheese
½ cup canned *canellini* (white pinto beans),
   drained
½ cup canned *ceci* (garbanzo beans), drained

2 Tbs. salt
2 cups orecchiette
   freshly grated parmigiano cheese to taste
   (optional)

In a large saucepan, heat the oil, add the onion, celery, and carrots, and sauté over low flame until the onion turns light golden. Over a medium low flame do all the following: add the potatoes and zucchini, mix well, add 2 cups of the water, and cook, covered, for 10 minutes. Now add the spinach, basil, parsley, and salt and pepper. Stir well and cook, covered, for 10 more minutes. Add the wine, bouillon cubes, and marinara sauce. Mix well, cover, and cook for 5 minutes. Add the remaining 6 cups water. Stir well, add the cheese, cover, and let simmer for 30 minutes. Add the pinto beans and *ceci*, cover, and cook for another 5 minutes. Turn off the flame and let stand.

In another pot of 3 quarts salted boiling water, cook the pasta for 6 minutes. Drain and add to the minestrone. Let it all simmer together for 5 minutes, stirring well. (If the soup is too dry, you may add more water at this point.) Turn off the flame and let stand for a few minutes before serving. Serve in soup bowls. You may add additional cheese over each serving if you wish.

*Serves 6 to 8.*

During Antony's first year we lived in Rome, and Roberto had to travel a great deal. I didn't want Antony to forget his father, so every morning when he awoke I took him to the living room for a visit to his daddy's photo and he seemed to enjoy it a great deal. In fact, our visits to his father's photo became a highlight of his day and when I began feeding him solid foods I would say, "Antony, let's have lunch with Daddy today," and in we went. One day, while feeding him this new dish of Straciatella, I talked to him constantly about his daddy and told him all about Roberto's letters. I was so proud that I managed to get him to finish his first solid food.

When the day approached for Roberto's return to Rome, I was a little worried. Poor Roberto was anxiously coming home to see his son, and it was possible his son wouldn't recognize him. The day arrived, and we went to the airport with Antony's godfather. At the airport, I must confess I was nervous, but thank God, as soon as Antony saw his father approaching he became terribly excited. He reached out to him and Roberto took him in his arms. What a happy reunion, and what a moment of triumph for me. I had no idea that our daily lunches under Roberto's photo would pay off in this manner. I also learned that it is never too early to begin communicating with your children.

—Flora

# 52. Straciatella alla Romana

## (Roman Egg and Cheese Soup)

4 cups chicken soup (or 5 cups water with 2 chicken bouillon cubes)
½ lb. acini di pepe
1 Tbs. salt
½ lb. spinach (fresh or frozen), cooked and finely chopped (optional)
2 eggs, beaten with a pinch of salt
2 Tbs. freshly grated parmigiano cheese
1 Tbs. finely chopped fresh parsley
pinch of ground nutmeg
salt and pepper to taste

Place your chicken soup in a 4- or 5-quart pot over a low flame. (If you are using bouillon cubes, bring 5 cups water to a boil and add the 2 chicken bouillon cubes, along with some of the parsley.)

In a medium pot, cook the pasta in one quart salted boiling water, but be sure it is very *al dente*. Drain the pasta and add it to the chicken broth, over a low flame. (If you are using the spinach, add it now.) Add the eggs, stirring continuously, then add 1 tablespoon of the cheese, the remaining parsley, and the nutmeg. Don't let this cook too long. As soon as the eggs coagulate, remove the pot from the flame. Serve hot in warmed soup bowls or dishes and sprinkle remaining cheese over each serving.

*Serves 4.*

## 53. Minestrone Campagniolo

### (Minestrone Country Style)

¼ cup olive oil
1 medium yellow onion, chopped
2 slices bacon, diced
½ dried red chili pepper, crushed
1 lb. sweet Italian sausage, fried, drained, and sliced
pinch of dried rosemary
½ cup dry white wine
½ lb. cabbage, chopped
½ lb. swiss chard, chopped
1 tsp. dried basil
1 large potato, peeled and diced into bite-sized cubes
4 to 6 cups water
salt to taste

2 Tbs. salt
2 cups ditalini

In a large saucepan, heat the oil and add the onion, bacon, and chili pepper. Sauté until the onion wilts and the bacon is crisp. Add the sliced sausage and rosemary. Mix well. Add the wine, cover, and let simmer for 5 minutes. Add the cabbage, swiss chard, basil, and potato, stirring well. Add the water and salt to taste and mix well. Bring to a boil, then lower the flame and let simmer for 30 minutes. Turn off the flame and let stand.

In 2 quarts salted boiling water, cook the pasta until very *al dente* (about 6 minutes). Drain and add to the minestrone. Let simmer all together for 5 more minutes, mixing well. Turn off the flame and let stand, covered, for a few minutes before serving. Serve in soup bowls.

*Serves 6 to 8.*

# ACT FOUR:

---

# FISH

Fish is one of the most abundant natural resources of Italy. The country has an enormous coastline and if you were to travel up and down both coasts, you would find countless quaint fishing villages in addition to the big city ports like Genoa, Naples, and Bari. It seems there is an endless variety of fish one can find in Italy and most of the time it is fresh. And Italians do love their fish. Where else but in Italy do people eat fresh sardines and fresh anchovies, fried to a crisp turn or marinated to a zesty flavor?

Now fish, or *pesce*, is not to be confused with *frutti di mare*, fruit of the sea. *Frutti di mare* is seafood, clams, mussels, lobsters, scungilli, calamari (squid), shrimp, and scampi. Oh, yes, shrimp *and* scampi. They are really not the same. Scampi are favorites from the Adriatic, more like a prawn than shrimp, and they are really a different type of shellfish. In the United States, for some strange reason, scampi has come to mean broiled shrimp in garlic and olive oil. The shrimp in this country are fine, but some restaurants import scampi from Italy because the scampi from the Adriatic are considered the best in the world.

Neopolitans, who are probably the biggest pasta eaters in all of Italy, also adore their fish. In the harbor of Santa Lucia, on the Bay of Naples, there are several famous seafood restaurants. When you walk into Zia Teresa's or the Mediterraneo or the Transatlantico, there is always an abundance of fresh fish on display next to the colorful antipasto table. In addition to making their famous Zuppa di Pesce or Fritto Misto, the Neopolitans use a variety of fish and seafood in their pasta recipes.

We hope you enjoy the ones we have selected for you.

## 54. Spaghetti con Vongole

### (Spaghetti with White Clam Sauce)

**Sauce:**

⅓ cup olive oil
2 cloves garlic, very finely sliced
⅓ cup clam juice
½ tsp. dried oregano
   freshly milled black pepper to taste
¼ tsp. salt
1 can (7½ oz.) minced clams
2 Tbs. chopped fresh Italian parsley

1 lb. spaghetti
3 Tbs. salt

In a medium skillet, heat the oil and sauté the sliced garlic until it barely begins to color. Remove from the flame and let cool. Add the clam juice, oregano, ¼ teaspoon black pepper, and ¼ teaspoon salt and let simmer for 5 minutes. Add the minced clams, with their juices, stirring well, then cook, uncovered, for 8 to 9 minutes, so that the liquid will reduce a bit. Stir in 1 tablespoon of the parsley and mix well.

Cook the spaghetti in 5 to 6 quarts salted boiling water until *al dente*. Drain well and place in a large serving bowl. Add half the clam sauce, toss well, then place the remaining clam sauce on top of the pasta and sprinkle the remaining parsley on top. More black pepper may be added, and it is ready to serve. Use warmed soup bowls.

*Serves 4 to 6.*

With this dish of pasta, I'm going to take you to one of my favorite cities, Venice (Italy, not California). I was making my very first film, playing the female lead in *La Gondola del Diavolo* (*The Devil's Gondola*). I'm sure most everyone has seen or read about the beautiful sights of Venice: the piazzas, the canals, the cathedrals, and the picturesque bridges. There are fabulous restaurants to be found everywhere.

My sister had accompanied me to Venice and one day the director invited us to lunch at a marvelous place called Malamocco. It's a funny sounding word and I wish I knew the meaning of it, but it was simply the owner's name. Feruccio Malamocco . . . even the names sound musical in Italy. As soon as we sat down the director insisted we try the Perciatelli con Tonno; it was *speciale*. I was a little reticent, to say the least. How could tuna and pasta be that good? I tried to talk my way out of it, but my sister convinced me to try at least a forkful. As soon as I tasted it, I was in heaven. I ordered a full portion and to everyone's surprise, I had a second order too!

I barely toddled back to the set, and once in my dressing room, I suddenly realized I had to get back into a fifteenth-century costume. It took both my sister and the wardrobe lady to literally squeeze me into the dress. They finally got me into it, but I remember I could hardly breathe. We rehearsed the scene and then began to shoot it. Just as the leading man took me in his arms, I reached up to embrace him and the entire seam of the costume split open!

It was the most expensive lunch the production had ever bought me. It took two hours to repair the dress and the director never again suggested pasta to me, even though we made three pictures together.

—Flora

## 55.  Perciatelli con Tonno

### (Tubular Spaghetti with Tuna)

**Sauce:**

3  Tbs. olive oil
1  medium yellow onion, chopped
2  scallions, finely chopped
2  cans (6½ oz.) tuna fish (packed in oil)
3  cups marinara sauce (page 9)
3  Tbs. chopped fresh parsley
1  tsp. coarsely ground black pepper

1  lb. perciatelli (or linguini)
3  Tbs. salt

In a 5- or 6-quart pot (about the size of a dutch oven), heat the oil, then add the onion and scallions, and sauté until golden brown. Stir in the tuna, with its oil, breaking it into small pieces. Cook over a medium flame for 2 to 3 minutes. Cool for a moment, then add the marinara sauce, 1 tablespoon of the parsley, and the pepper. Simmer for 5 minutes, turn off the flame, and let stand.

Cook the pasta in 5 to 6 quarts salted boiling water until *al dente*. Stir and test frequently (all tubular macaroni are a bit tricky and must be checked). Drain thoroughly (the tubular macaroni retains water). Place in a large warmed serving bowl and gently add the sauce. Sprinkle the remaining parsley over the pasta and serve in warmed soup dishes or bowls. No cheese, please!

*Serves 4 to 6.*

**B**ucatini con le Acciughe is a well-known Neopolitan dish. You will find it in the southern regions of Italy, such as Naples, Calabria, and Sicily. A lot of the southern recipes use anchovies and *sarde* (fresh sardines). One time we were in Naples visiting some of my father's family and on the way back to Rome we stopped off at one of Naples' famous seaside restaurants, Zia Teresa's. Flora and I were enjoying the Bay of Naples and waiting for the waiter to take our order. Suddenly I was approached by one of the local *scugnizzi*, a street urchin, who made it a habit of begging from American tourists. I must have had my American shoes on that day because he spotted me immediately. When I saw what a dirty face he had I said, "If you want some money, you have to wash yourself first." He thought for a second, then raced from the table and I wondered if he understood my fractured Italian. (I still spoke with an American accent in those days.) We watched him run around the dock and dive into the water. He splashed around a bit, then ran back to us with his hair slicked down and his open palm extended. He said, "Now I'm clean, can I have the money?" Well, Flora and I laughed so heartily at this ingenious method of instant cleaning that I dug down and gave him a handful of coins. Flora said, "Maybe his poor family will eat well tonight," but quick as a flash, he joined two or three of his young friends and began gambling with them, "heads or tails" with the coins. He was having a good time and so were we. Neopolitans learn very early to live by their wits and have a good time.

—Robert

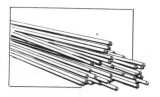

## 56. Bucatini con le Acciughe

### (Macaroni with Anchovies)

**Sauce:**

¾ cup olive oil
3 cloves garlic, cut in half

8  anchovy fillets (packed in oil)
3  cups canned (or fresh) plum tomatoes, diced
½  cup dry white wine

1½  cups unseasoned bread crumbs

1¼  lb. bucatini (or spaghettini)
3  Tbs. salt
5  Tbs. chopped fresh parsley

In a medium skillet, heat the oil, reserving three tablespoons for later. Brown the garlic and discard. Add the anchovies and let simmer until they are almost melted. Cool the oil for a moment while you put the tomatoes and juice in a blender at the lowest speed for only a few seconds. Add the tomatoes to the oil, bring to a boil, then let simmer for 20 minutes. Add the wine, cover, and let simmer for 3 more minutes, then turn off the flame and let stand. In a small skillet, heat remaining oil over low flame and fry or toast the bread crumbs until golden brown.

Cook the bucatini in 8 to 9 quarts salted boiling water until *al dente*. Drain thoroughly (bucatini are tubular and tend to retain a lot of water). Place in a large warmed serving bowl, add the sauce and bread crumbs, and toss well with a wooden fork and spoon. Sprinkle generously with parsley and serve immediately in warmed soup bowls.

*Serves 6.*

Naturally, we found this recipe on the Isle of Capri, often referred to as one of the jewels of Naples by the proud Neopolitans. The other jewel is the Isle of Ischia. In the summer of 1971 I was invited, along with several other actors, to receive an award from the Chamber of Commerce of the Isle of Capri. Flora was delighted we were going to spend a weekend in Capri because she had been in love with the place ever since she had made her second movie there, *L'Isola del Sogno* (*Island of Dreams*).

The awards were to be made on a Saturday night at an outdoor theater. Flora and I were seated in the first row with an old friend of ours, Corbett Monica and his wife. We had just come from dinner and were waiting for the show to start. After a half hour of waiting, we realized something was wrong because off to the right of the stage several people were gathered, talking rather loudly with arms waving in the air, very much in the Italian style. After another half hour of waiting one of the organizers of the show came to me and explained that their master of ceremonies, an Italian actor named Alberto Lupo, had missed the hydrofoil from Naples and they weren't sure when he'd arrive. I could see by the look in his eyes that he was in desperate need of help but was too shy to ask. I offered to M.C. the show until Lupo arrived and he almost kissed my hand. Flora thought I was a bit loco to accept such a chore, but I assured her I could manage. I introduced several acts, I even brought Corbett Monica on stage and he did a pantomime routine the audience found very funny. Finally Lupo showed up for the second half of the show. We received our awards and the evening was over.

The next morning, I found out how well the show had gone. When I walked down the quaint streets of Capri, all the shop-keepers came out to shake my hand. I was very impressed by the warmth of these people because they told me I had saved their evening for them. It's a beautiful island. Don't miss it if you're ever in the neighborhood. Very romantic, too!

—Robert

## 57.  Spaghettini alla Caprese

### (Spaghettini Capri Style)
**Sauce:**

     ½  cup olive oil
     1  can (20 oz.) plum tomatoes
     1 or 2  pinches salt
     1  oz. anchovy fillets (packed in oil)
     ½  cup canned tuna fish (packed in olive oil)
     ½  cup dry white wine
    10  black Sicilian olives (oil cured), pitted

     2  Tbs. salt

1½ lb. spaghettini
¾ cup grated mozzarella cheese
freshly milled black pepper to taste

In an 8-inch skillet, heat the olive oil. Process the tomatoes in a blender at the lowest speed for just a few seconds, then add them to the skillet (away from the burner, so that if any oil spills over, it won't flare up at you). Add a pinch or two of salt, cover, and let cook briskly over medium-high flame for about 15 minutes.

Meanwhile place the anchovies and tuna in a food processor. (If you have no processor, then the old-fashioned way will do, slicing the anchovies finely and then placing both the anchovies and the tuna in a small bowl and mixing them well with a fork.) The oil from the anchovies and tuna should keep the mixture moist enough, but if necessary, you may add a few drops of olive oil. When the tomatoes have finished cooking, add the anchovy-tuna mixture, the wine, and olives to the skillet and let simmer for 5 minutes. (Like most sauces, this can be made anytime during the day, and you can let it stand in your refrigerator until dinner.)

To 7 to 8 quarts boiling water add the 2 tablespoons salt and then your spaghettini. This type of pasta is very fine and will cook much more quickly than the regular spaghetti, so keep your eye on it. Stir frequently with a wooden fork and test it often until it is cooked *al dente*. Drain well and dress immediately with the sauce (which should be heated). Sprinkle the mozzarella over the pasta, toss again with wooden forks, then add a generous sprinkling of freshly milled black pepper. Toss once more and serve at once. Your guests should be at the table, or the spaghettini will turn into a ball of dough. Serve in warmed soup bowls.

*Serves 6 to 8.*

One afternoon a group of us drove down to Naples from Rome for the gala opening of *South Pacific*. We were invited by two of our oldest and dearest friends, Lydia and Rossano Brazzi. Rossano was starring in the film and we were happy to go along and share his joy. Betty and Mario Lanza were also going to join our party, but at the last minute Mario couldn't make it. He had gone to a spa for a crash diet because he and Roberto were going to do a film together in a couple of weeks and he wanted to get into shape.

After the opening of *South Pacific*, which was very gala indeed, attended by all the local luminaries and a great many of the NATO commanders stationed in Naples, our group went to supper and had a memorable evening. It was one of Brazzi's best roles which added to the festivities, ending with Rossano and Roberto singing Neopolitan love songs. What a night to remember. During dinner, Betty Lanza had seen a large platter of pasta and calamari go by, a big favorite in Naples. She asked me what it was and after I explained she invited us to her home the following evening to cook some for her. She said she was anxious to get back to Rome to listen to a taped radio show Mario had made. It was only being heard in Rome the next evening, and Mario had dedicated the show to her. We agreed and Roberto and I joined her and her family in Rome. After we prepared the pasta and calamari, we listened to Mario's voice over the radio during the rest of dinner. It was a wonderful evening, and for two nights in a row it proved once again how well pasta and good music go together.

—Flora

## 58. Linguini con Calamari

### (Flat Macaroni with Squid)

**Sauce:**

½ cup olive oil
1 *peperoncino* (dried red chili pepper), broken in half
2 cloves garlic, cut in half
1 large yellow onion, sliced
1 lb. calamari
½ tsp. dried rosemary

1 cup marinara sauce (page 9)
½ cup dry white wine

1 lb. linguini
3 Tbs. salt
¼ cup chopped fresh parsley

In a large skillet, heat the oil and sauté the chili pepper and garlic until browned, then discard the garlic. Add the onion and sauté for about 10 minutes, or until golden.

Wash the calamari, then cut the heads in half and the bodies into rings. (You do this by cutting across the squid, rather than lengthwise, making cuts about 1 inch apart. When they begin to cook, they curl into rings.) Add the calamari to the onions, then crumble the rosemary as you add it. Sauté for about 6 minutes. Add the marinara sauce and wine and mix well. Cover and let simmer for 40 to 50 minutes (depending on the size of the squid—the larger ones need more cooking time). Turn off the flame and let stand.

Cook pasta in 5 to 6 quarts salted boiling water until *al dente*. Drain well and place in a large warmed serving bowl. Add the sauce, tossing well with a wooden fork and spoon. Sprinkle the parsley over the pasta and serve immediately in warmed soup dishes.

*Serves 6.*

This recipe is a big favorite in Naples, and that's exactly where we had it. We were almost at the end of the tour with the musical, *La Padrona Di Raggio Di Luna*. After finishing our tour of Sicily, we stopped in Naples for a ten-day return engagement before going back to Rome for the final playing date.

We were giving a Saturday night performance and the cast could tell it was going to be a noisy one. Just before the curtain went up, the audience seemed noisier than the usual Saturday night crowd, until someone told us what was going on out front. Alberto

Sordi, who was then Italy's top box-office draw, had just arrived. That was enough to excite any audience, but he was sitting in the company of Ginger Rogers and her new husband, the handsome Jacques Bergerac. It was small pandemonium, but once the curtain went up, the audience quieted down. Some of the cast, however, could not. Particularly our soubrette, who said, "Mamma mia, how am I going to dance in front of Ginger Rogers?" I replied, "Easy, just think of me as Fred Astaire." That broke the tension and it turned out to be one of the best shows we had ever done.

After the show, Sordi brought Ginger and Jacques back-stage and they visited with everyone. Ginger hadn't seen me since *Guys & Dolls*, several years before. The producers then invited them to supper with us. Flora and I had often seen Sordi in Rome, but we surely never expected to see Ginger Rogers in Naples. It was one of Flora's most thrilling evenings, meeting Ginger, and the Linguini con Frutti di Mare was a fitting climax to a perfect evening.

—Robert

## 59. Linguini con Frutti di Mare

### (Linguini with Seafood)

Sauce:

½ cup olive oil
1 *peperoncino* (dried red chili pepper), broken in half
3 cloves garlic, cut in half
½ tsp. dried rosemary
1 tsp. pickled capers
¼ cup chopped fresh parsley
8 Little Neck clams, well scrubbed
8 mussels, well scrubbed
12 medium shrimp, shelled, deveined, and cut in half
8 calamari, cleaned and sliced

¾ **cup dry white wine**
2 **cups marinara sauce (page 9)**

1½ **lb. linguini**
3 **Tbs. salt**

In a medium skillet, heat all but 2 tablespoons of the oil, add the red chili pepper and garlic, and sauté until golden brown, then discard the garlic. Add the rosemary, crushing it with your fingers. Add the capers and 1 tablespoon of the parsley. Simmer for about 2 minutes, turn off the flame, and let stand.

Place the remaining oil in a 5- or 6-quart pot, along with 1 cup of water. Add the clams and mussels and cook over a medium flame until the shells open. Remove the meat from the shells and add the clam and mussel meat, along with the juices, to the other ingredients in the skillet. Stir in the shrimp and calamari and sauté, uncovered, for 15 minutes. Add the wine and marinara sauce, cover, and let simmer for 15 minutes.

Cook the pasta in 8 to 9 quarts salted boiling water until *al dente*. Drain thoroughly, place in a warmed serving bowl, and dress with the sauce, tossing everything together with a wooden fork and spoon. Serve immediately in warmed soup dishes or bowls.

*Serves 8.*

If you're a member of the film industry in Italy, as I was before I met Roberto, sooner or later you have to go to the Venice Film Festival. I made three pictures for Scalera Films, so the studio invited me to go as their guest. I shall never forget my stay at the magnificent Excelsior Hotel, which is on the Lido di Venezia, overlooking the Adriatic Sea. Venice is always beautiful, but in late August and early September it seems to take on an extra sparkle because of the festival—perhaps from the many film stars who come from all over the world for this important event. Add their glow to the glow of the city and it becomes very exciting for the local citizenry. During the course of the festival I met many European and American film stars, but two actors remain very vivid to me because of a party we attended. It was the end of the festival and the Conte Volpi Di Misurata, who was a government official, decided to give a closing night party. He lived in a huge house on the Grand Canal. If it wasn't *the* most gorgeous home I had ever seen, it certainly was *one* of the most gorgeous. Such antiques and paintings I have rarely seen, and it seemed as if the entire festival were there. I'm sure there were more than a hundred guests.

When it came time for the buffet supper I found myself in a small group with Kirk Douglas and the late Zachary Scott. The pasta was the main attraction and they both asked me what the dish was. When I told them that Fettuccine alla Veneta contained shrimp and sole, they lost interest. Through an interpreter, since my English was very limited in those days, I was able to convince them to try it. They did, and to my surprise and the host's delight, they tried it again and again and again. Once more, a great dish of pasta helped international relations. And it happens every day, all over the world.

—Flora

## 60.   Fettuccine alla Veneta

### (Noodles Venetian Style)

1½  medium yellow onion, sliced
2  Tbs. sweet butter
1  cup dry white wine
1  tsp. salt
1½  lb. lemon sole fillets, cubed (about ½-inch pieces)

½ lb. shrimp, shelled, deveined, and cut into
   small pieces
1 cup light cream
½ tsp. white pepper
   pinch of curry powder (optional)
1 lb. fettuccine

3 Tbs. salt
2 Tbs. freshly grated parmigiano cheese
2 Tbs. freshly grated Romano cheese

In a large skillet, sauté the onions in 1 tablespoon of the butter till they are light golden brown. Add the wine and ½ teaspoon of the salt. Stir in 1 pound of the fish cubes and half of the shrimp, and cook for 10 minutes. Put the rest of the raw fish and shrimp in a blender with 2 tablespoons of the broth from the cooked onion-fish mixture. Blend to a paste, remove from the blender, and fold in the cream, pepper, and curry powder. Stir well into a smooth paste. Let this simmer over a low flame until the mixture thickens a little. Add the remaining ½ teaspoon salt and stir until smooth.

Cook the fettuccine in 5 to 6 quarts salted boiling water until extra *al dente.* Drain thoroughly.

Butter a large baking dish. Spread a layer of the fettuccine on the bottom, then a layer of the cooked fish cubes and shrimp, then a layer of the smooth paste. Repeat until all the fettuccine, fish and shrimp, and paste have been used up. Mix the two cheeses together and sprinkle them on top of the pasta, making this your last layer. Dot with the remaining tablespoon butter. Place under the broiler until the top becomes browned, about 8 to 10 minutes. Serve in warmed platters.

*Serves 8.*

# 61. Spaghettini con Vongole al Sugo Rosso

## (Spaghettini with Red Clam Sauce)

**Sauce:**

¼ cup olive oil
3 cloves garlic, minced
½ large yellow onion, chopped
1 can (2 lb. 3 oz.) Italian plum tomatoes
1 tsp. dried oregano
2 bay leaves
½ tsp. salt
½ dried red chili pepper
   coarsely ground black pepper to taste
1 can (10 oz.) minced clams
½ cup dry white wine (or Chablis)

1 lb. spaghettini (preferably imported)
3 Tbs. salt

In a medium skillet, heat the oil and sauté the garlic and onions over a low flame until lightly golden. Process the tomatoes in a blender for only a few seconds at the lowest speed, then add them to the garlic and onion over a moderate flame. Add the oregano, bay leaves, salt, chili pepper, and black pepper and let simmer for 20 minutes. Add the clams, with their juices, stirring well, and let simmer, uncovered, until the sauce thickens a bit, about 5 to 6 minutes. Add the wine, cover, and let simmer for 3 or 4 more minutes.

Cook the spaghettini until *al dente*, in 5 to 6 quarts salted boiling water. Drain very thoroughly. Place in large serving bowl. Add half the sauce, remove bay leaves, and toss well. Save the remaining sauce for the table. Serve in warmed soup bowls.

*Serves 4 to 6.*

## 62. Linguini con Cozze

### (Linguini with Mussels)

**Sauce:**

½  cup olive oil
2  cloves garlic, finely sliced
½  dried red chili pepper
1½  lb. mussels, shelled and cooked (featured this way in many fish markets)
    salt to taste
2  Tbs. chopped fresh parsley
½  cup dry white wine (or Chablis)

1  lb. linguini
3  Tbs. salt
    freshly milled black pepper to taste

In a medium skillet, heat the oil and sauté the garlic and chili pepper until the garlic is golden, and let cool. Add the mussels, salt to taste, and 1 tablespoon of the parsley. Let simmer for 5 minutes. Add the wine, cover, and let simmer for 5 more minutes.

Cook the linguini in 5 to 6 quarts salted boiling water until *al dente.* Do not drain thoroughly, but remove the pasta with a spaghetti fork (or regular fork) and place in a large serving bowl. Add half the sauce and toss well. Then add the remaining sauce on top of the pasta and sprinkle with the remaining parsley. Serve immediately in warmed soup bowls, making an even distribution of the mussels for each serving. Some freshly milled black pepper may be added for extra flavor.

*Serves 4 to 6.*

## 63. Penne al Pescatore

**(Penne, or Mostaccioli, Fisherman's Style—Shrimp and Scallops)**

Sauce:

⅓  cup olive oil
3  cloves garlic, cut in half
½  lb. medium shrimp, shelled, deveined, and
    boiled, cut in half
½  lb. bay scallops
1  tsp. salt
    freshly milled black pepper to taste
2  Tbs. chopped fresh parsley
1  can (2 lb. 3 oz.) Italian plum tomatoes
5 or 6  fresh basil leaves, chopped
¼  cup dry sherry

1  lb. penne (or mostaccioli)
3  Tbs. salt

In a large skillet, heat the oil and sauté the garlic. When the garlic turns golden brown, discard. Add the shrimp, scallops, salt, pepper, and 1 tablespoon of the parsley and let simmer for 5 or 6 minutes. In the meantime, process the tomatoes in a blender for a few seconds at the lowest speed. Add the tomatoes to the skillet, bring to a boil, then let simmer slowly for 25 minutes. Now add the basil and sherry, cover, and let simmer for 3 more minutes. Turn off the flame and let stand.

Cook the pasta until *al dente* in 5 to 6 quarts salted boiling water. Drain thoroughly and place in a large serving bowl. Add a generous amount of the sauce, some more black pepper, and toss well. Add more sauce, placing the shrimp and scallops on top of

the pasta. Sprinkle the remaining parsley on top and serve immediately in warmed platters.

*Serves 4 to 6.*


# 64.   Spaghettini con Scungilli

## (Thin Spaghetti with Scungilli)

**Sauce:**

1   can (10 oz.) scungilli (conch)
½   cup olive oil
2   cloves garlic, minced
1   can (1 lb. 12 oz.) Italian plum tomatoes
2   bay leaves
½   tsp. coarsely ground black pepper
¼   cup sherry
8   fresh basil leaves, chopped (or 1 tsp. dried)

1   lb. spaghettini
3   Tbs. salt
1   Tbs. chopped fresh parsley

Rinse the scungilli a couple of times, using first hot, then
cold water. Drain and dice them. In a large skillet, heat the oil.
Brown the garlic and discard it. Add the scungilli and sauté until
browned. While the scungilli are cooking, mash the tomatoes in a
bowl, by hand or with a fork. Add the tomatoes, bay leaves, and
pepper to the browned scungilli. Let simmer for 20 minutes, then
add the sherry and basil. Cover and let simmer for a few more
minutes.

Cook the spaghettini until *al dente* in 5 to 6 quarts salted
boiling water. Drain thoroughly and place in a large serving bowl.
Add half the sauce, remove bay leaves, and toss well. Sprinkle the
parsley generously on top of the pasta. Serve immediately, bringing the remaining sauce to the table.

*Serves 4 to 6.*

# 65. Spaghetti con le Sarde

## (Spaghetti or Linguini with Sardines)

Sauce:

2 heads fresh fennel (anise) (about 1 cup leaves)
½ cup olive oil
1 large yellow onion, chopped
3 cloves garlic, chopped
2 cans (6 oz.) tomato paste
  salt to taste
1 tsp. coarsely ground black pepper
4 cups water
2 cans (7½ oz.) boneless and skinless sardines,
  drained and halved
1 cup dried unseasoned bread crumbs

1 lb. spaghetti (or linguini)
3 Tbs. salt

Remove the leaves and part of the stems from the fennel, wash, then cook them in 7 quarts boiling water about 5 to 6 minutes. Remove the fennel and reserve the water for the pasta. Finely chop the cooked fennel stems and leaves. In a large skillet, heat 5 tablespoons of the oil and sauté the onion and garlic until golden. Add the tomato paste, salt, and pepper. Mix well and sauté for a couple of minutes. Add the chopped fennel and the 4 cups water. Bring to a boil, then let simmer for 40 minutes. Add the sardines and cook for a few more minutes. In a small skillet, heat the remaining oil and add the bread crumbs. Slowly brown them, being careful not to burn them.

Cook the pasta in the saved fennel water, adding 3 tablespoons salt, until *al dente*. Drain well and place the pasta in the large skillet containing the sauce. This should be done over a moderate flame, mixing well as you go. Add the browned bread crumbs and continue mixing. A few more turns of your pepper mill would go well here. After a couple of minutes, turn off the flame. Cover and let stand for a minute or two before serving.

Serve directly from skillet in warmed soup bowls.

*Serves 4 to 6.*

NOTE: The bulbs of the fennel can be washed, quartered, and served at the end of the meal. It is a great digestive.

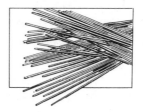

# 66. Vermicelli con Olio ed Acciughe

## (Vermicelli with Oil and Anchovies)

### Sauce:

½ cup olive oil
3 cloves garlic, 2 whole and 1 finely sliced
½ dried red chili pepper (optional)
1 tsp. dried oregano
1 oz. anchovy fillets, drained and minced

1 lb. vermicelli
3 Tbs. salt
1 Tbs. chopped fresh parsley

In a small skillet, heat the oil and sauté the garlic (and chili pepper if desired) until light golden. Discard the 2 cloves that are not sliced and add the oregano. Mix in the anchovies. Turn off the flame and let stand.

Cook the pasta in 5 to 6 quarts salted boiling water until *al dente*. (Remember to keep your eye on the vermicelli, as they can overcook very easily.) Drain and place in a large serving bowl. Add the sauce, tossing with a wooden fork and spoon. Sprinkle with the parsley and serve in warmed soup bowls.

*Serves 4 to 6.*

## 67. Spaghettini Amalfitani

(Spaghettini Amalfi Style)

Sauce:

¾ cup olive oil
2 cloves garlic, finely sliced
1 anchovy fillet, minced
6 black Sicilian olives, pitted and chopped
6 large green olives, pitted and chopped
2 tsp. pickled capers
½ tsp. dried oregano
1 dried red chili pepper, broken into 2 pieces
1 can (6½ oz.) tuna fish (packed in olive oil)

1 lb. spaghettini
3 Tbs. salt
1 Tbs. chopped fresh parsley

In a medium skillet, heat the oil and sauté the garlic until light golden. Add the anchovy, and when it has melted, add the olives, capers, oregano, and chili pepper. Sauté for 4 or 5 minutes over a medium flame. Meanwhile, place the tuna in a dish with its oil. Using a fork, mash it into small pieces, then add to the skillet. Mix well and let simmer for 7 or 8 minutes. Turn off the flame and let stand.

Cook the pasta until *al dente* in 5 to 6 quarts salted boiling water. (Watch it closely. Thin spaghetti cooks rather quickly.) Stir it often so that it doesn't stick together. Drain and place in a large serving bowl. Pour the sauce over it and toss well. If it seems at all dry, you may add 1 or 2 additional tablespoons oil before serving. Sprinkle the parsley over the pasta and serve in warmed soup bowls.

*Serves 4 to 6.*

## 68.  Fettuccine Verdi con Gamberetti

### (Green Noodles with Shrimp)

¾  lb. medium shrimp
1  tsp. salt

1  lb. green fettuccine (you may use packaged,
    but homemade is preferred, page 5)
3  Tbs. salt
¼  lb. sweet butter
    coarsely ground black pepper to taste
    (we like a lot)
1  Tbs. chopped fresh parsley
½  cup heavy cream, warmed
    chopped fresh parsley to taste

Cook the shrimp in 1 quart salted boiling water, 3 to 4
minutes, or until they turn pink. Drain, shell, devein, and cut them
in half.

Cook the pasta in 5 to 6 quarts salted boiling water until
extra *al dente*, and drain well.

You may do the next step in a large skillet over a low
flame, but we prefer a chafing dish, tableside. Melt the butter, add
the shrimp, pepper, and some of the parsley, and sauté for 3 minutes. Add the fettuccine and toss well with the shrimp and butter.
Add the cream and blend into the pasta just before serving. Sprinkle
some parsley and black pepper over each serving. No cheese,
please. Serve in warmed soup bowls.

*Serves 4 to 6.*

# ACT FIVE:

# MEAT

Now we come to the "act" we call beautiful but dangerous. Beautiful, because these are some of the most delicious recipes of all. Dangerous, because you could go completely mad about them and eat a little too much.

You will note that when Italians use meat in their sauces, it is with much more imagination than meatballs. In the following recipes you will find ground veal, pork, and beef. You will find prosciutto, ham, and bacon, or sausage, salami, and mortadella. If you look hard enough, you will also find chicken livers. So you see, a great variety of meats are used. Very often these recipes become the main course because of the abundance of meat in the sauce. We leave that up to your discretion. Generally, however, when you serve a large main course of meat or fish, the pasta, or *primo piatto*, should be very simple.

How often we have tried to follow this simple rule when dining out in Rome, but somehow it never seemed possible. Maybe because the pasta course was a very moderate portion, meant to be followed by a meat or fish course. Or perhaps because dining in Rome always consumed at least two hours and if we were in the company of two or three other couples, it meant up to three hours at dinner: the antipasto, the pasta, the main course, the *contorni* (side dishes of vegetables), salad, fruit, and dessert. And let's not forget the vino and espresso. An evening well spent. We hope you enjoy the following recipes as much as we enjoyed those wonderful Roman evenings.

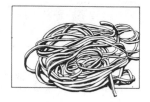

## 69.   Taglierini Campagnioli

### (Homemade Thin Noodles, Country Style)

Sauce:

- 3  Tbs. olive oil
- 2  scallions, finely chopped
- ¾  cup dry white wine
- ½  lb. chicken livers, washed and diced
- 3  Tbs. sweet butter
- 3  pinches dried sage
   salt and freshly milled black pepper to taste

- 1  lb. taglierini (page 5; green taglierini, page 28)
- 3  Tbs. salt
- ¼  cup freshly grated parmigiano cheese

In a medium skillet, heat the oil and sauté the scallions until lightly golden. Add the wine and let simmer for a few minutes. Add the chicken livers, butter, sage, and salt and pepper, and stir well. Cook over a moderate flame for 10 to 12 minutes. Turn off the flame and let stand.

Cook the pasta in 5 to 6 quarts salted boiling water until *al dente*. (Homemade noodles have to be watched and stirred more often than commercial pasta.) Drain and place in a large serving bowl. Add the sauce and toss well. Add the cheese and toss once more. Add a liberal amount of freshly milled black pepper. Serve immediately in warmed soup bowls.

*Serves 4 to 6.*

While preparing this book, we suddenly realized that pasta dishes are like favorite songs. You can always recall a certain occasion when you sang or danced to the song, just as we recalled this special occasion when we had Spaghetti alla Carbonara. Flora and I had tasted this dish literally hundreds of times, at home and in restaurants all over Italy, but we shall never forget this occasion.

I was doing a Broadway show, *What Makes Sammy Run?*. It was a Saturday afternoon and between shows, Flora and I were invited to the Hilton Hotel, right next door to the theater. An old friend of ours from Rome, Ugo Tognazzi, was in town promoting his latest film and they were giving him a press party at the Hilton. Besides being one of Italy's top actors, Ugo is also a great cook. He decided he would contribute to the party by cooking one of his favorite dishes for all the guests. As often happens in New York, over 300 people showed up. Ugo had an enormous suite with a full-size kitchen, and as soon as he had greeted us at the door, with the ritual kisses on both cheeks, he dragged us into the kitchen. He seemed a bit perturbed but well organized. On one counter top were all the ingredients: a large bowl with beaten eggs, another large bowl with grated parmigiano, and a large platter with pieces of the fried bacon. We got the first clue to his worries when he complained, "Doesn't this American water ever come to a boil?" Then we discovered what was wrong. When Ugo saw the large turnout of guests, he asked the hotel to send up some large pots for cooking. They sent up large pots all right, but they were the commercial pots used in their restaurant kitchens, and the stove in the suite was an ordinary apartment stove. The small burners just never got hot enough to heat the water in the large copper pots. Ugo was livid! Flora suggested he cook in smaller pots and serve four or five people at a time rather than twenty as he originally intended.

Unfortunately, my time between shows ran out, so I left Flora at the party and went to the theater to do the evening performance. After the show, I returned to the Hilton. Poor Ugo was still in the kitchen cooking and Flora still hadn't eaten. We decided the best thing to do was to wish him well and after more hugging and kissing, we went down to dinner, real Roman style . . . at 11:30 P.M. We will never forget that day and neither will Ugo.

Whenever we see him in Rome we ask him if the water has come to a boil yet.

—Robert and Flora

# 70. Spaghetti alla Carbonara

## (Spaghetti Charcoal Vendor's Style)

- 2 eggs
  pinch of salt
- 1 Tbs. freshly grated parmigiano cheese
- 2 Tbs. olive oil
- 2 scallions, finely chopped
- ¾ lb. lean bacon, diced (very lean for cholesterol-watchers—we care about your health)
- 1 lb. spaghetti
- 1 Tbs. salt
- 1 Tbs. sweet butter
- ¼ lb. parmigiano cheese, freshly grated
- 2 Tbs. coarsely ground black pepper

In a small bowl, beat the eggs with a pinch of salt and the 1 tablespoon cheese. Let stand.

In a small skillet, heat the oil and lightly brown the scallions. Add the bacon and sauté until well done but not too crisp. Turn off the flame and let stand.

Cook the spaghetti in 5 to 6 quarts salted boiling water (only 1 tablespoon salt is needed here) until a moment less than *al dente*. (You will be reheating it in a few minutes when you blend in the other ingredients.) Drain well. Place the butter in the spaghetti pot over a low flame and return the spaghetti to the pot. Mix in the bacon and scallions, stir well with a wooden fork, and add the eggs. Keep tossing constantly over a low flame while adding the ¼ pound cheese and the pepper. Within a couple of minutes, at the first sign of the eggs cooking, the pasta will be done. Your guests should be at the table because this is really an *espresso* dish. Serve from the pot into warmed pasta bowls.

*Serves 4 to 6.*

This is one of the most famous dishes in Rome and you will find it in almost any restaurant there. They all serve it with great pride and each says theirs is *speciale*. The dish gets its name from the little town of Amatrice in the Sabina hills that form part of the surrounding countryside of Rome, known as Lazio. One of the most colorful things of Lazio are their soccer games with Rome. You see, Rome is a city in the region of Lazio, and when the two teams get together, the rivalry is bigger than the old Giant and Dodger games in New York or Brooklyn.

In the late fifties I was making an Italian movie with Gina Lollobrigida and Vittorio Gassman. One Sunday afternoon in April, Flora thought we would enjoy the day by attending one of the Rome-Lazio games. It was an absolutely gorgeous day and overhead was one of the bluest skies I had ever seen. Everything was rather calm, though noisy, until one of the teams scored a point. Then it was as though a civil war had erupted. Before we knew it, we were quite involved. I tried to remain impartial, but Flora was a devoted Lazio fan, something I hadn't discovered till that afternoon. The "civil war" lasted till the end of the game, and I really thought someone might be killed. Suddenly, the game was over and tempers cooled off. We were invited to join the group sitting around us at an early dinner. We arrived at a restaurant with a group of about twenty, where all the losers consoled themselves with Bucatini all'Amatriciana. Double portions and lots of wine! Pasta has power to soothe the savage breast.

—Robert

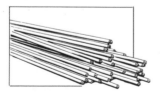

## 71. Bucatini all'Amatriciana

### (Bucatini Amatrice Style)

**Sauce:**

   1 can (1 lb. 12 oz.) plum tomatoes
   ¼ lb. salt pork, diced

2½ Tbs. olive oil
1 medium yellow onion, chopped
6 oz. lean bacon, diced
½ cup dry white wine
½ tsp. salt (or to taste)
½ tsp. freshly milled black pepper

3 Tbs. salt
1½ lb. bucatini
1 cup freshly grated Pecorino cheese (or Romano cheese)

Place the tomatoes in a blender, process at the lowest speed for a few seconds only, and let stand. In a large skillet, sauté the salt pork until lightly browned on all sides. Remove the pork and set aside, discarding the grease. Place the oil in the skillet, add the onions and sauté until light golden. Add the bacon and sauté until the bacon begins to take on color. Add the wine and the salt pork and let simmer for a few more minutes. Add the tomatoes and season with salt and pepper. (You may not need the salt because of the pork and bacon, but the Romans like it well seasoned.) Cook over a medium-high flame for 15 minutes, covered, then turn off the flame and let stand.

To cook the pasta, bring 8 or 9 quarts of water to a fast boil. Add the 3 tablespoons salt, then add the bucatini. Stir frequently with a wooden fork and cook the pasta until *al dente*. Drain well. (This is a tubular pasta and will retain water unless well drained.) Place in a large warmed serving bowl and toss with half the sauce. Sprinkle generously with the cheese, reserving some of it for the table. Serve immediately, along with the remaining sauce and cheese. Serve in warmed soup bowls.

*Serves 6 to 8.*

**O**ne of the magical things about living in Rome is that you are within a few hours drive of some of the most interesting and historical places in Italy. One such place is Assisi, where I took Roberto one weekend. It is difficult to describe Assisi, especially the many spiritual vibrations one receives when visiting there. To me, the most inspiring place is the Church of Santa Maria degli Angeli and the Porziuncola. Translated, Porziuncola means "a little portion of earth." A small chapel was built there in the fourth century, and it was later rebuilt and restored by Saint Francis in the thirteenth century. In the garden is the legendary rosebush. The legend is that Saint Francis of Assisi threw himself upon the rosebush to overcome a strong temptation, and from that moment on, the rosebush remained thornless.

After our visit there, we stayed overnight at the Hotel Subasio on a hillside overlooking a vast panorama of the Umbrian countryside spread out before our eyes like a green carpet. The regions of Le Marche and Umbria, incidentally, are world renowned for their cooking and also for some of the best sausages in Italy. That's why part of our dinner that night was Spaghetti con Salsicce e Piselli. What a treat to end a beautiful day. But if you should ever get to Assisi, don't miss the church of Santa Maria degli Angeli and the Porziuncola. That's the real treat.

—Flora

## 72. Spaghetti con Salsicce e Piselli

### (Spaghetti with Sausage and Peas)

Sauce:

- 3 sweet Italian sausages
- ½ cup olive oil
- ½ tsp. dried rosemary
- ¾ cup dry white wine
- 2 scallions, chopped
- ½ lb. canned tiny peas, drained
- ½ tsp. salt (or to taste)

1   **Tbs. chopped fresh parsley**

1   **lb. spaghetti**
3   **Tbs. salt**
1   **tsp. coarsely ground black pepper (or to taste)**
6   **Tbs. freshly grated parmigiano cheese**
2   **Tbs. sweet butter (optional)**

In a small saucepan, boil the sausages for 5 or 6 minutes to eliminate the excess grease. Use enough water to cover sausages. Remove the skins, break the sausage meat into small pieces, and let stand. In a large skillet, heat a bit more than half the oil (about 5 tablespoons), add the rosemary and sausage meat, and sauté until the meat is browned. Add ½ cup of the wine, cover, and let simmer for 5 minutes. Turn off the flame and let stand.

In a small saucepan, heat the remaining oil and add the scallions. When golden brown, add the peas, salt, parsley, and the remaining ¼ cup wine. Cover and let simmer for 2 to 3 minutes. Then pour all of this into the skillet that has the sausage. Cover and let simmer for 3 minutes. Turn off the flame and let stand.

Cook the pasta in 5 to 6 quarts salted boiling water until *al dente.* Drain and place it in the large skillet containing the sauce. Toss until well mixed with a wooden fork and spoon, adding the pepper and cheese as you go. If it seems a bit dry, you may add the butter while tossing the pasta over a low flame. Serve in warmed soup dishes or bowls.

*Serves 4 to 6.*

**W**hat a joyous memory this dish brings to mind. Roberto was busy on a film in Hollywood and our son Antony, then only nine, was chosen to play one of the leads in the TV pilot of the famous movie *Three Coins in the Fountain.* The added joy was that the pilot was going to be shot in Rome and we hadn't been back there for a couple of years. I had to accompany Antony to Rome, and Roberto would join us later. One day, the company was shooting exteriors in the heart of the city, at the Fontanella Borghese. There is a well-known restaurant nearby, La Fontanella, which is always terribly crowded for lunch. I explained to Antony where he was to join me when the company broke, and I went on ahead. Fortunately, I was able to get a nice table and was calmly looking over the menu while waiting for Antony to arrive. Before long, there was quite a commotion at the front door of the restaurant, and when I looked up, I saw Antony being brought to me, accompanied by a policeman and a waiter. I thought my heart would stop until they explained what had happened. Antony was about to enter the restaurant but was stopped by the waiter. You must understand that his part in the film called for him to be dressed as a Roman street urchin. The waiter thought he was coming in to beg from the customers and tried to chase him away. He wouldn't believe there was someone inside waiting for a street urchin, so he called a policeman. Antony kept insisting in two languages that his mother was in there waiting for him. When they discovered that Antony was telling the truth, there were apologies from everywhere. The owner didn't know how to make up for the waiter's gaff, so he suggested we try the specialty of the day, on the house. Thank goodness Antony ate a hearty meal. Even though there was a moment of fear, it still remains one of our joyous memories.

—Flora

## 73.  Fettuccine alla Pastora

### (Shepherd-Style Noodles)

    1  cup sweet Italian sausage meat (optional)
    1  lb. fettuccine (packaged or homemade, page 5)
    3  Tbs. salt
    2  cups ricotta (about 1 lb.)
       salt and freshly milled black pepper to taste
    ¾  cup freshly grated Pecorino cheese

If you choose to use the sausage meat, it should be crumbled (out of the skin) and sautéed over low flame for 6 to 7 minutes or until browned.

Cook the fettuccine in 5 to 6 quarts salted boiling water

until *al dente*. Drain thoroughly, reserving ½ cup of the water, and place in a large warmed serving bowl.

In a small bowl, mix the ricotta with a little salt and pepper and whip until smooth. Add the reserved water left over from cooking the pasta and mix well. Now add the ricotta mixture to the pasta in the serving bowl, along with the cheese and some pepper to taste. Toss gently for a moment, then add the sausage meat. Toss well with a wooden fork and spoon and serve immediately in warmed soup dishes.

*Serves 6 to 8.*

## 74. Linguini con Mentuccia

### (Linguini with Mint)

**Sauce:**

  3  Tbs. sweet butter
  2  cloves garlic, crushed
  ½  lb. sweet Italian sausage
  ½  cup dry white wine
  1  cup fresh mint, chopped
  1  tsp. dried oregano

  1  lb. linguini
  3  Tbs. salt

In a medium skillet, melt the butter, add the crushed garlic, and sauté until golden. Remove the sausage meat from the skins, crumble, and place into the skillet. Sauté until the meat is browned. Remove the garlic, add the wine, mint, and oregano, and mix well. Cover and let simmer for 6 to 7 minutes. Turn off the flame and let stand. (For a variation, you can use ½ sweet and ½ hot sausage.)

Cook the linguini in 5 to 6 quarts salted boiling water until *al dente*. Drain well, and place in a large serving bowl. Add the sauce and toss well. Serve immediately in warmed soup bowls.

*Serves 4 to 6.*

## 75. Fettuccine al Tricolore

### (Fettuccine with Three Colors)

*Fettuccine al Tricolore is a very colorful as well as a very tasty dish. If ever you should want to establish the fact that you are serving an Italian dinner, this is the perfect primo piatto, or first course. The three colors of the Italian flag are very evident. The carrots are red, the mushrooms are white, and the peas are green. Of course, the taste is exquisite or, as the Italians say, squisito.*

2   medium carrots
2   Tbs. olive oil
4   Tbs. sweet butter
2   scallions, chopped
4   thin slices, prosciutto, diced
1   can (8 oz.) early peas
4   large mushrooms, sliced
¼   cup sherry

1   lb. fettuccine, packaged or homemade (page 5)
3   Tbs. salt
6   Tbs. freshly grated parmigiano cheese
     coarsely ground black pepper to taste

Parboil the carrots about 10 minutes, then chop them. In a large skillet, heat the oil and butter, add the scallions and prosciutto, and sauté for 5 minutes. Add the carrots, peas, and mushrooms and sauté for 5 more minutes. Add the sherry, cover, and let simmer for a few minutes, then turn off the flame and let stand.

Cook the fettuccine in 5 to 6 quarts salted boiling water until *al dente*. Drain well and put into the skillet with the other ingredients. Add the cheese and pepper, tossing gently over a low flame for a couple of minutes. Serve directly from the skillet or a chafing dish. Serve in warmed flat dishes or soup bowls.

*Serves 4 to 6.*

# 76.  Mostaccioli al Andrea

## (Mostaccioli Andrea Style)

*Our very good friend Andrea, owner of Andrea's restaurant in the heart of Rome, cooked this dish for us so often that he finally gave us the recipe as a wedding gift.*

### Sauce:

½  lb. sweet Italian sausage
½  lb. hot Italian sausage
 3  Tbs. olive oil
 2  scallions, chopped
    pinch of dried rosemary
 1  large slice mortadella, minced
½  cup dry white wine
 1  can (2 lb. 3 oz.) Italian plum tomatoes

 1  lb. mostaccioli
 3  Tbs. salt
 6  Tbs. freshly grated parmigiano cheese
 8  fresh basil leaves, chopped

Parboil the sausages to remove the excess grease. Remove the skins and crumble the meat. In a large skillet, heat the oil and lightly brown the scallions. Add the sausage meat, rosemary, and mortadella. Over a medium flame, sauté the meats until browned. Add the wine, cover, and let simmer for 10 minutes. Meanwhile, process the tomatoes in a blender at a low speed for just a few seconds. Add the tomatoes to the skillet, mix well, bring to a boil, then let simmer for 30 minutes over a medium flame, stirring at intervals.

Cook the pasta in 5 to 6 quarts salted boiling water until *al dente* and drain well. Place in a large serving bowl. Pour the sauce over it, sprinkle with cheese, and toss well. Dot the pasta with the fresh basil leaves and serve immediately in warmed serving bowls.

*Serves 4 to 6.*

# 77. Fettuccine alla Bolognese

## (Noodles with Bolognese Sauce)

1 lb. fettuccine, packaged or homemade (page 5)
3 Tbs. salt
4 Tbs. butter
½ cup freshly grated parmigiano cheese
3 cups Bolognese sauce (page 12)

Cook the fettuccine in 5 to 6 quarts salted boiling water, stirring often to keep from sticking. Drain well and place the pasta in a skillet over a low flame or in a chafing dish tableside. Add the butter and toss well. Add half of the grated cheese right onto it and toss again. Serve in soup bowls, with 3 tablespoons hot Bolognese sauce topping each serving. Place remaining sauce and cheese at the table. Serve in warmed soup bowls.

*Serves 4 to 6.*

# 78. Fettuccine Perilli

## (Fettuccine Perilli Style)

*Here's a recipe given to us by Francesco Perilli, who has one of the most beautiful outdoor garden restaurants just a couple of blocks behind the American consulate in Rome. We have watched Perilli graduate from waiter to captain to maître d' to, finally, the owner of one of Rome's finest restaurants. He gave up this recipe especially for our book. We hope you will enjoy it as much as we do.*

**Sauce:**

¼ lb. sweet butter
½ lb. lean pork, finely diced
1 tsp. salt
   coarsely ground black pepper to taste
½ cup dry white wine
3 cups marinara sauce (page 9)
1 can (8 oz.) early peas
6 medium fresh mushrooms, sliced
2 Tbs. chopped fresh parsley

1 lb. fettuccine, packaged or homemade (page 5)
3 Tbs. salt

In a large skillet, melt half the butter over medium-low flame, add the pork, and sauté until browned. Add the salt, pepper, and wine. Cover and let simmer for 5 minutes. Add marinara sauce and let simmer for 30 minutes. In a small skillet or saucepan, melt the remaining butter, add the peas, mushrooms, and 1 tablespoon of the parsley. Cook for about 5 or 6 minutes, then blend into the pork-tomato sauce. Let simmer for 10 more minutes, then turn off the flame and let stand.

Cook the fettuccine in 5 to 6 quarts salted boiling water until *al dente*. Drain well and place in a large serving bowl. Pour half the sauce over the pasta and toss well. Sprinkle the remaining parsley over the top. The remaining half of the sauce should be spooned over each serving.

*Serves 4 to 6.*

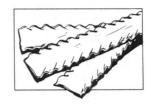

## 79.  Lasagnette al Prosciutto

### (Broad Noodles with Prosciutto)

1  lb. lasagnette
3  Tbs. salt
1  Tbs. oil

8  thin slices Italian prosciutto, cut into julienne strips
9  Tbs. sweet butter
1  can (8 oz.) early peas, drained
½  cup freshly grated parmigiano cheese
     coarsely ground black pepper to taste
¼  cup heavy cream (optional)
     salt to taste (optional)

Cook the lasagnette in 5 to 6 quarts salted boiling water until *al dente*, adding the oil to keep the noodles from sticking. Drain thoroughly.

In a large skillet over a low flame, or a chafing dish, sauté the prosciutto in 1 tablespoon of the butter until crisp. Add the peas and sauté for 2 more minutes, mixing well. Add the remaining butter, and while it is melting, add the pasta and toss well. Add the cheese and pepper and continue to toss well with wooden forks, so that the butter is evenly distributed. Add the cream if you wish, tossing until it warms. Taste for salt and add if you desire. Serve in warmed soup bowls with a dash of pepper over each serving.

*Serves 4 to 6.*

# ACT SIX:

# BAKED AND/OR STUFFED

We like to think of these nineteen recipes as the *crème de la crème*, the "elite," the recipes for festive occasions. Both of us remember that most of these recipes were usually served on holidays or some special event such as a birthday or anniversary. Particularly the lasagne or manicotti. They lend themselves so well to a special dinner because they actually have a special look about them. They do take a bit longer to prepare than some of the other recipes in this book, but they are without doubt worth every extra minute. With some, you can even prepare part of the recipe the day or evening before you plan on serving it. In that way you are not too rushed or too tired on the day of your dinner.

The great thing about these dishes is that very often there are leftovers. We store them very carefully in the refrigerator and when we use them two or three days later, they seem to be tastier than the first time. We usually keep a jar of marinara sauce in the refrigerator as well. The trick is to use these leftovers on a night when you don't have too much time for cooking. All you have to do is reheat the sauce and the pasta, prepare a salad, and finish with some fresh fruit. It helps your budget, takes care of your appetite, and you've saved a lot of time.

This is a very festive dish and the recipe always reminds us of another festive occasion. The first time we tasted a similar dish was in Taormina, Sicily. We really didn't go there for the food; after all, we were going on our honeymoon to one of the most beautiful and romantic spots in all the world. But sooner or later, you do have to eat. Taormina is situated high on a hill, overlooking the beautiful blue Mediterranean. Whether you are up high in the town proper, or down below at the beach, you often feel as though you have left this planet for the astral world. It may have been because of the honeymoon, but Flora and I both felt the same way, and food was of secondary importance.

One day, one of the local fishermen spotted us on the beach. After some friendly chitchat, he realized we were a couple of tourists. He suggested a great restaurant on a hillside overlooking the sea. The poor guy meant well but we practically gave him the brush. Who had time for restaurants on a honeymoon? Later that evening, we realized we both needed some "refueling" and decided to try the fisherman's suggestion. It turned out to be a delightful evening, not only for the Ziti al Forno, but also for the guitar player who sang many of our favorite Italian love songs. That's how we found this basic recipe to add to our collection. We only wish that someday you too can visit Taormina and have the thrilling and exciting time we had.

—Robert

# 80. Ziti al Forno

### (Baked Ziti)

1½  lb. ziti
4  Tbs. salt

1½  lb. ricotta
2  recipes marinara sauce (page 9)

½ lb. early peas
3 oz. Italian salami, sliced, then cut into ¼-inch squares
1 cup cubed mozzarella cheese (¼-inch cubes)
¼ lb. freshly grated parmigiano cheese
1 tsp. coarsely ground black pepper (or to taste)
2 eggs, beaten
10 to 12 fresh basil leaves, chopped

Cook the ziti in 8 to 9 quarts salted boiling water until very *al dente* (not more than 6 minutes, as they are to be baked for 20 minutes later). Stir often with a wooden fork.

While the pasta is cooking, mix the ricotta and half of the marinara sauce together in a large bowl until well mixed. Drain the pasta well and put it into the bowl. Mix all together with a wooden fork and spoon, adding the peas, salami, mozzarella, and half of the parmigiano cheese. Add half of the remaining sauce and reserve remainder for table. Keep mixing gently.

Now place the mixture into a large buttered baking dish. Pour the eggs over the entire surface of the pasta. Generously sprinkle the chopped basil leaves over the entire surface and sprinkle the rest of the parmigiano cheese over the surface too. The dish is now ready for the oven; however, it can stand in your refrigerator for several hours this way if you want to prepare it in advance.

When ready to dine, preheat oven to 400 degrees and bake for 15 minutes, then place it under the broiler for an additional 5 minutes. When a golden crust has formed on the surface, your Ziti al Forno is ready. When you serve the individual portions, pour some reserved sauce over each.

*Serves 8 to 10*, depending on whether the ziti is used as a *primo piatto* or as a main course.

**M** y sister, Ann, and Flora have become very close or, as Flora puts it, "Now I have a sister in Roma and a sister in New York."

When Flora first tasted Ann's manicotti, she said she had never tasted manicotti so good in her whole life. And how could it be so very light and fluffy? After cross-examining Ann, we finally discovered her secret. She does not use pasta dough. Ann makes this recipe with crepes and serves it on very special occasions such as Easter, Christmas, or New Year's. We are delighted to pass this recipe on to you with Ann's compliments. Happy feasting!

—Robert

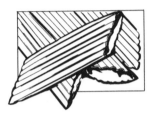

## 81.  Manicotti all'Anna

### (Crepes Filled with Ricotta)

**Crepes:**

3  cups all-purpose flour
3  cups water
4  eggs
   pinch of salt

   olive oil

**Filling:**

3  lb. ricotta
1  Tbs. chopped fresh parsley
½  cup freshly grated parmigiano cheese
1  large egg (or 2 small)
   salt and pepper to taste
½  lb. mozzarella cheese, cubed

2  recipes marinara sauce (page 9)

½  cup freshly grated parmigiano

To make the crepes, mix the crepe ingredients together well until they reach a consistency like batter. Brush a 6-inch skillet with olive oil, and when the pan is good and hot, pour ¼ cup (4 tablespoons) of the batter into the pan, tilting the pan back and forth so that the batter spreads evenly. When the top of the crepe is dry, flip it into a dish and repeat as many times as the mixture will allow (about 50). (Note: You need grease your skillet only one time.) The crepes can be made days ahead and stored in the refrigerator with plastic wrap between each crepe.

To make the filling, combine the ingredients for the filling in the order given until everything is well mixed.

Preheat the oven to 400 degrees.

To make the manicotti, lay out about 6 of the crepes before you and place a tablespoon of the ricotta mixture on the center of each. Gently roll the crepes, leaving the ends open. If the ricotta has been properly placed in the center of the crepe, it will not leak out of the ends. Repeat process until all ingredients are used up.

Cover the bottom of a large baking pan with marinara sauce, then place your manicotti side by side in as many rows as your pan holds. You will probably need to use two baking pans. Spread some more sauce over the top of the manicotti, then sprinkle generously with the parmigiano. Bake for 20 to 25 minutes. Serve hot on flat plates or warmed soup bowls. Bring remainder of sauce and parmigiano cheese to table.

*Serves 12.*

# 82. Farfalle con Polpettine al Forno

## (Baked "Bow Ties" with Tiny Meatballs)

    1   lb. ground beef
    ½   yellow onion, very finely chopped
    3   Tbs. seasoned bread crumbs
        salt
        freshly milled black pepper
    2   eggs, beaten
    1   Tbs. chopped fresh parsley
    6   fresh basil leaves, chopped (or ½ tsp. dried)
    ¼   cup milk
    6   Tbs. olive oil
    2   cloves garlic, cut in half
        pinch of dried rosemary
    ½   cup dry white wine
    1   can (2 lb. 3 oz.) Italian plum tomatoes

    1   lb. farfalle
    3   Tbs. salt
    9   Tbs. freshly grated parmigiano cheese

Thoroughly mix together the beef, the onion, the bread crumbs, 3 tablespoons cheese, ½ teaspoon salt, ½ teaspoon pepper, 1 of the eggs, the parsley, the basil, and the milk. Roll into tiny meatballs, about the size of marbles. In a large skillet, heat the oil and brown the garlic and discard it. Add the meatballs and rosemary and over a medium flame brown the meat on all sides. Add the wine, cover, and let simmer for 5 minutes. Meanwhile, in a medium bowl, crush the tomatoes either by hand or with a fork. When the meatballs have simmered in the wine, add the tomatoes and more salt and pepper to taste. Mix well and let cook, covered, over a low flame for 30 minutes, stirring at intervals.

Preheat the oven to 400 degrees.

Cook the pasta in 5 to 6 quarts salted boiling water until very *al dente*. Drain well and place in a large bowl. Pour half the sauce with the meatballs over the pasta, add 6 tablespoons cheese, and mix well. Place some of the remaining sauce in the bottom of a baking dish, pour in the pasta, and pour the remaining sauce on top. Spoon the other beaten egg over the pasta. Bake for 10 minutes, then set under the broiler for 10 more minutes, or until a light crust forms on top. Serve immediately.

*Serves 6.*

# 83. Lasagne Campagniolo al Forno

## (Baked Lasagne, Country Style)

1 lb. lasagne, packaged or homemade (page 5)
3 Tbs. salt
2 Tbs. oil

½ lb. boiled ham, diced
1 lb. mozzarella cheese, diced
1 lb. ricotta
4 hard-boiled eggs, sliced
2 recipes ragù sauce (page 10)
¼ cup freshly grated parmigiano cheese
   freshly milled black pepper to taste

Cook the pasta in 5 to 6 quarts salted boiling water, to which you have added the oil to keep the pasta from sticking, until very *al dente*. Remove the pasta with a slotted spoon and place on a large cloth to dry.

Preheat oven to 400 degrees.

Butter a large baking dish and lay down a layer of the pasta, then scatter a layer of diced ham, mozzarella, ricotta, and eggs, then cover with ragù sauce. Sprinkle on some of the parmigiano and pepper. Repeat the process until all the ingredients are finished, reserving some of the sauce for the final layer (as well as about 2 cups for serving at the table). Bake for 20 minutes. Serve immediately in flat warmed dishes. Add more sauce at the table.

*Serves 8 to 10.*

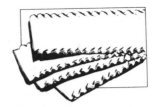

## 84. Lasagne alla Napoletana

### (Baked Lasagne, Roberto's Family Style)

2  Tbs. olive oil
1  medium yellow onion, chopped
2  cloves garlic, minced
1  lb. lean pork, diced
   salt and pepper to taste
½  cup dry white wine
1  can (35 oz.) Italian plum tomatoes
1  can (6 oz.) tomato paste
1  Tbs. chopped fresh parsley
8  fresh basil leaves, chopped (or 1 tsp. dried)
1  lb. lasagne, packaged or homemade (page 5)
3  Tbs. salt
1  Tbs. olive oil
¼  lb. Italian salami, diced
1  lb. ricotta
¼  cup freshly grated parmigiano cheese

In a large skillet, heat the oil, add the onion and garlic, and sauté until light golden. Add the pork and the salt and pepper and brown the meat over medium-high flame. Add half the wine, cover, and let simmer for 10 minutes. Meanwhile, process the tomatoes in a blender at the lowest speed for just a few seconds. Add the tomatoes, tomato paste, and parsley to the skillet and bring to a boil, covered, over a high flame. After 5 minutes reduce the flame and let simmer for about 1 hour. Add the remaining wine and the basil, cover, and let simmer for 5 more minutes. Turn off the flame and let stand.

Cook the pasta in 5 to 6 quarts salted boiling water, to which you have added the oil to keep the pasta from sticking, until *al dente.* Remove with a slotted spoon and place on a large cloth to dry.

Preheat oven to 400 degrees.

In the bottom of a large baking dish spread a spoonful or two of the sauce, then lay down a layer of lasagne, cover with some of the salami, ricotta, parmigiano, and spoon some more of the sauce over it. Repeat this process until all the ingredients are finished. Cover with generous spoonfuls of sauce and bake for 20 minutes. Serve immediately in warmed flat plates.

*Serves 6 to 8.*

## 85. Rigatoni alla Fontina

### (Rigatoni with Fontina Cheese)

1  lb. rigatoni
3  Tbs. salt

6  Tbs. sweet butter
½  pound fontina cheese, thinly sliced
2  pinches ground nutmeg
1  cup freshly grated parmigiano cheese
liberal amount of coarsely ground black pepper (or to taste)

Preheat oven to 400 degrees.

Cook the rigatoni in 5 to 6 quarts salted boiling water until extra *al dente* (they will finish cooking in the oven). Drain well and place them in a large bowl.

Add 4 tablespoons of the butter, ½ cup of parmigiano, and nutmeg and mix well until all the pasta is coated. In a buttered baking dish, make a layer of the pasta, a layer of the fontina cheese, sprinkle with the parmigiano, and repeat the process until the pasta is used up, ending with a layer of the fontina on top. Sprinkle with parmigiano and black pepper and dot with the remaining butter. Bake for 15 minutes, or until the cheese is well melted. May be served on flat plates.

*Serves 4 to 6.*

## 86. Lasagne alla Siciliana

### (Baked Lasagne, Flora's Family Style)

4 Italian sausages (2 sweet, 2 hot)
½ cup olive oil
1 lb. fresh mushrooms, sliced
2 cloves garlic, minced
2 pinches dried rosemary
½ cup dry white wine
1 can (35 oz.) Italian plum tomatoes, chopped
1 can (6 oz.) tomato paste
½ tsp. dried oregano
8 fresh basil leaves, chopped (or ½ tsp. dried)
  salt and pepper to taste

1 lb. lasagne, packaged or homemade (page 5)
3 Tbs. salt
1 Tbs. olive oil
1 lb. ricotta
¾ lb. mozzarella cheese, thinly sliced
½ cup freshly grated parmigiano cheese

Parboil the sausages to remove the excess grease, then remove their casings and crumble the meat. In a small skillet, heat 2 tablespoons of the oil and over a low-medium flame and sauté the mushrooms for 8 to 10 minutes. Turn off the flame and let stand. In a large skillet, heat the remaining oil and brown the garlic. Add the sausage meat and rosemary and brown over medium-high flame. Add the wine, cover, and let simmer for 10 minutes. Turn off the flame and add the tomatoes, tomato paste, oregano, basil, and salt and pepper. Mix well, bring to a boil, and after boiling for 10 minutes let simmer for 1 hour, stirring often.

Cook the pasta in 5 to 6 quarts salted boiling water, to which you have added the oil to keep the pasta from sticking, until very *al dente*. Remove the pasta with a slotted spoon and place on a large cloth to dry.

Preheat oven to 400 degrees.

In a buttered baking dish (you may spread a couple of spoonfuls of sauce instead of buttering), spread a layer of lasagne, a layer of sauce with sausage meat, and a layer of ricotta, mozzarella, and mushrooms. Sprinkle the parmigiano cheese generously and repeat the process until all the ingredients are finished. Top the pasta with a liberal spoonful of sauce. Bake for 25 minutes. Serve hot in warmed flat dishes.

*Serves 6 to 8.*

# 87. Lasagne Verde Bolognese

## (Green Lasagne, Bolognese Style)

4 cups flour
4 eggs
1 cup cooked spinach, drained and chopped
¼ cup spinach juice (reserved from cooking spinach)

3 Tbs. salt
1 recipe ragù sauce (page 10)
1 recipe béchamel sauce (page 13)
½ cup freshly grated parmigiano cheese

Place the flour on a level workboard. Make a well in the center of the flour and add the eggs. Work the flour and eggs into a dough, then add the spinach and spinach juice and work and knead into a smooth, fine dough. Roll out the dough very thin and cut it into 5- or 6-inch squares. Let dry on a large cloth for at least 1 hour.

Parboil the pasta about 5 to 6 minutes in 6 quarts salted boiling water until extra *al dente* and drain.

Preheat oven to 400 degrees.

In a buttered baking dish, lay down a layer of pasta, a layer of ragù sauce, a layer of pasta, and a layer of béchamel sauce. Repeat the process, ending with a layer of the béchamel. Sprinkle generously with the cheese. Bake for 20 minutes, or until the top begins to brown. Serve immediately in warmed flat plates.

*Serves 4 to 6.*

## 88. Canelloni di Pasta Verde

### (Baked Green Canelloni)

3 Tbs. salt
1 recipe pasta verde (page 28)
1 Tbs. oil

Filling:

1 lb. ricotta
12 thin slices lean prosciutto, diced
2 Tbs. chopped Italian parsley
2 eggs, beaten
1 clove garlic, minced
1 cup freshly grated cheeses, Romano and
parmigiano mixed
1 tsp. salt
coarsely ground black pepper to taste

3 Tbs. sweet butter, melted
2 cups béchamel sauce (page 13)
2 cups Bolognese sauce (page 12)

Cut the dried pasta dough into 4-inch squares. In 6 quarts salted boiling water, to which you have added the oil to keep the pasta from sticking, cook 4 or 5 pasta squares at a time. Cook the pasta squares for about 5 minutes, then remove with a slotted spoon and place on a linen kitchen towel or large cloth to dry.

Meanwhile, preheat oven to 400 degrees.

When the pasta squares are all cooked, place the ricotta in a large bowl. Add the prosciutto, parsley, eggs, garlic, cheeses, salt, and pepper, mixing well as you add each ingredient. When thoroughly mixed, place a generous spoonful of the ricotta filling on each pasta square, then gently roll each one into a tube about 1½ to 2 inches in diameter. Place them side by side in a buttered baking dish. Spoon some melted butter over each one. Spoon the béchamel sauce, then the Bolognese sauce over the canelloni. Bake for 15 minutes. Serve in warmed flat dishes.

*Serves 4 to 6.*

# 89. Lasagne con Cavolfiore

## (Baked Lasagne with Cauliflower)

*Prepare the following ingredients to use between the layers of pasta:*

1½  lb. ricotta, crumbled
  4  eggs, beaten
  3  pinches ground nutmeg
  ¾  cup freshly grated parmigiano cheese

  1  lb. lasagne, packaged or homemade (page 5)
  3  Tbs. salt
  1  Tbs. olive oil
  1  large head cauliflower, diced and sautéed
     salt and pepper to taste

In a small bowl, cream the ricotta with 2 of the beaten eggs, the nutmeg, and 2 tablespoons of the parmigiano cheese.

Cook the pasta in 5 to 6 quarts salted boiling water, to which you have added the oil to keep the pasta from sticking, until very *al dente*. Remove the pasta with a slotted spoon and place on a large cloth to dry.

Preheat oven to 400 degrees.

In a buttered baking dish, place a layer of pasta, a layer of cauliflower, a layer of the ricotta-parmigiano mixture, and salt and pepper. Repeat this process until all the ingredients are finished, the last layer being lasagne. Spoon the remaining 2 beaten eggs over the pasta. Bake for 20 minutes.

This dish may be served either hot or cold—for instance, hot one day and cold the next.

*Serves 6 to 8.*

## 90. Ravioli con Ricotta

### (Ravioli with Ricotta)

**Filling:**

1 lb. ricotta
¾ cup freshly grated parmigiano cheese
1 egg, beaten
½ tsp. salt
½ tsp. freshly milled black pepper
1 Tbs. chopped Italian parsley
3 pinches ground nutmeg

1 recipe ravioli dough (page 5)
3 Tbs. salt

4 cups ragù sauce (page 10), heated
¾ cup freshly grated parmigiano cheese

In a medium bowl, place the ingredients for the filling and mix well until creamy smooth.

Roll out the dough until very thin and cut into strips 2 to 2½ inches wide. Place a teaspoon of filling on a strip of dough every few inches. Cover with another strip. With a ravioli cutter, cut the strips in between the spoonfuls of filling. (This cuts and seals at the same time.) Check for open edges, which can be sealed by pressing a fork tip over the dough. Place them on a cloth and let dry for at least 2 hours. (Some people let them dry overnight.)

Cook the ravioli in 6 to 7 quarts salted boiling water. Stir often, but gently, so as not to break the ravioli. When they rise to the top of the pot, they will be about done. Cook for 2 more minutes, then remove with a slotted spoon. Place in warmed serving bowls. Cover with hot ragù sauce, sprinkle with the parmigiano, and serve.

*Serves 4 to 6.*

## 91. Ravioli con Ricotta e Spinaci

### (Ravioli with Ricotta and Spinach)

Filling:

½ lb. ricotta
½ lb. spinach, cooked, drained, and chopped
1 egg, beaten
½ cup freshly grated parmigiano cheese
½ tsp. salt
½ tsp. freshly milled black pepper
1 tsp. chopped Italian parsley

1 recipe ravioli dough (page 5)
3 Tbs. salt

4 cups marinara sauce (page 9), heated
1 cup freshly grated parmigiano cheese

Place the ingredients for the filling in a medium bowl and mix well until creamy smooth.

Roll out the dough very thin (about ⅛ inch). Cut into strips about 2 to 2½ inches wide. Place half the strips on your workboard. Place a teaspoon of the ricotta filling on a strip of dough every few inches apart. Cover each strip with one of the reserve strips and cut with a ravioli cutter between the spoonfuls of filling. Seal the open ends with the tines of a fork. Place the ravioli on a large cloth and let dry for at least 2 hours (the longer the better).

Cook the ravioli in 6 quarts salted boiling water. Stir often but gently with a wooden spoon, so as not to break them open. When they rise to the top of the pot, they are about done, but let them cook a couple of minutes more. Remove with a slotted spoon and place in warmed soup bowls. Cover with marinara sauce, sprinkle with the parmigiano, and serve.

*Serves 4 to 6.*

## 92. Tortellini alla Bolognese

(Tortellini Bolognese Style)

Filling:

¼ lb. ground lean beef
¼ lb. ground lean pork
½ lb. ground turkey breast
3 thin slices lean prosciutto, minced
2 eggs, beaten with a pinch of salt
  pinch of dried sage
1 tsp. chopped fresh parsley
  salt to taste
  coarsely ground black pepper to taste
½ cup freshly grated parmigiano cheese

4 Tbs. sweet butter

1 recipe ravioli dough (page 5)
2 Tbs. salt
1 Tbs. oil

1 recipe Bolognese sauce (page 12), heated
½ cup freshly grated parmigiano cheese

Thoroughly mix together the ingredients for the filling until all is well blended. In a large skillet, melt the butter and sauté the ground meat mixture until lightly browned. Put the cooked meat through a grinder or food processor so that it is all finely ground.

Divide the ravioli dough in half and roll out into sheets about ⅛ inch thin. Cut into 2½- to 3-inch circles with an inverted glass or a cookie cutter. Place a level teaspoon of the filling on each circle of dough. Fold in half, making a half-moon, pinch the open ends together, then roll a bit more until you have a shape like a long finger. Then bring the ends together to form a ring. Sounds complicated but after doing a few, you'll become an expert. All it takes is a little patience. Place the tortellini on a large cloth and let dry for 2 to 3 hours before cooking.

Cook the tortellini in 6 to 7 quarts salted boiling water, to which you have added the oil to keep them from sticking together. Don't boil the water too violently, or the pasta may open. Cook until *al dente*, stirring often with a wooden spoon. Test for doneness before removing, then transfer with a slotted spoon to a large serving bowl. Pour some of the Bolognese sauce over the tortellini and toss gently with a wooden spoon. Serve in warmed soup bowls, sprinkling some cheese and some more of the sauce over each serving.

*Serves 4 to 6.*

# 93.　Agnellotti alla Panna

## (Agnellotti with Whipped Cream)

**Filling:**

1　cup ground veal (about ¼ lb.)
1　cup ground beef (about ¼ lb.)
6　thin slices Italian salami, minced
2　eggs, beaten
　　salt and freshly milled black pepper to taste
½　cup unseasoned bread crumbs
2　Tbs. freshly grated parmigiano cheese
1　Tbs. chopped fresh Italian parsley
　　pinch of dried rosemary

1　recipe ravioli dough (page 5)
3　Tbs. salt

**Sauce:**

¼　lb. sweet butter, melted
1　cup whipped cream (from aerosol can)
2　pinches ground nutmeg

6　Tbs. freshly grated parmigiano cheese
　　coarsely ground black pepper to taste

Mix together the ingredients for the filling until they are thoroughly blended.

Divide the ravioli dough in half, roll each half out, and stretch it until it is about ⅛ inch thin. Cut into circles about 2½ to 3 inches in diameter using a cookie cutter or an inverted glass. Place a level teaspoon of the filling in the center of each circle. Then fold each circle in half, making a half-moon. Press and seal the edges with the tines of a fork. Place them on a cloth and let dry for 2 to 3 hours before cooking.

Cook the agnellotti carefully in 6 to 7 quarts salted boiling water, stirring often with a wooden spoon, being careful not to let them open. When they rise to the top of the pot, they are almost done. Let them cook for a few more minutes, then remove to a large serving bowl with a slotted spoon.

You may prepare the sauce either before or during the cooking of the pasta. In a bowl, blend the melted butter into the whipped cream. Add the nutmeg. Then fold the sauce gently into the cooked pasta, adding more butter if it seems too dry. Transfer individual servings to warmed soup bowls and sprinkle each serving with parmigiano and pepper.

*Serves 6 to 8.*

## 94. Agnellotti al Ragù

### (Agnellotti with Ragù Sauce)

Filling:

5 oz. ground lean pork
5 oz. ground veal
5 oz. ground chicken breast
2 thin slices mortadella, minced
¼ cup parmigiano cheese
¼ cup unseasoned bread crumbs
2 eggs, beaten
1 Tbs. dried basil
½ tsp. crushed dried sage
2 pinches ground nutmeg
  salt and pepper to taste

1 recipe ravioli dough (page 5)

1 recipe ragù sauce (page 10), heated
8 Tbs. parmigiano cheese

Mix together all the ingredients for the filling until they are thoroughly blended.

Divide the ravioli dough in half and roll it out until ⅛ inch thin. Cut into circles of 2½ to 3 inches in diameter with an inverted glass or a cookie cutter. Place a level teaspoon of the filling in the center of each circle, then fold each one into a half-moon shape. Seal the edges with the tines of a fork. Place the agnellotti on a large cloth and let dry for 2 to 3 hours, or even overnight.

Cook the agnellotti in 8 quarts salted boiling water slowly and carefully, stirring often with a wooden spoon. When they rise to the top, let them cook for 3 more minutes. Test for doneness before draining. Remove with a slotted spoon and place in a large serving bowl. Add the ragù sauce, tossing gently with wooden spoons. Cover each serving with a tablespoon parmigiano cheese as you transfer it to a warmed soup bowl.

*Serves 6 to 8.*

## 95. Manicotti in Bianco

### (Manicotti with White Sauce)

Filling:

½ cup freshly grated Pecorino cheese
½ cup freshly grated parmigiano cheese
¼ lb. mozzarella cheese, diced
1 lb. ricotta
3 eggs, beaten
2 Tbs. chopped Italian parsley
3 pinches ground nutmeg
5 or 6 walnuts, chopped
½ tsp. salt
  coarsely ground black pepper to taste

4 to 5 cups béchamel sauce (page 13)

1 recipe manicotti dough (page 5)
3 Tbs. salt
1½ Tbs. olive oil

In a large bowl, blend together all the ingredients for the filling, mixing as thoroughly as possible. In a saucepan, heat the cheese sauce over a low flame.

Cut the manicotti dough into 4-inch squares and cook 4 or 5 at a time in 6 quarts salted boiling water, to which you have added the oil to keep the pasta from sticking. Remove the cooked pasta after about 5 minutes with a slotted spoon and place on a cloth or kitchen towel to dry.

Preheat oven to 400 degrees.

Place a generous spoonful of the ricotta filling on each square of pasta and gently roll the pasta into a tube about 1½ to 2 inches in diameter. Place the manicotti in a buttered baking dish, side by side, keeping them separated. Spoon the cheese sauce liberally over the manicotti. Bake for about 15 minutes. Serve on warmed flat plates.

*Makes about 12 manicotti. Serves 4 to 6.*

## 96.  Tortellini al Burro

### (Tortellini with Butter)

#### Filling:

    1  lb. ground turkey breast
    4  thin slices lean prosciutto, diced
   ½  cup freshly grated parmigiano cheese
   ½  cup unseasoned bread crumbs
   ½  tsp. chopped fresh parsley
      pinch of dried sage
    2  eggs, beaten
      salt to taste
      coarsely ground black pepper to taste

   ¼  lb. sweet butter

    1  recipe ravioli dough (page 5)
    3  Tbs. salt
    1  Tbs. oil

    1  cup heavy cream, warmed
   ½  cup freshly grated parmigiano cheese

Thoroughly mix together all the ingredients for the filling. In a medium skillet, melt half the butter and sauté the meat mixture for 5 or 6 minutes, or until lightly golden. Place the cooked meat in a grinder or food processor until it is finely ground.

Cut the ravioli dough into circles about 2½ to 3 inches in diameter, using a cookie cutter or an inverted glass. Place a level teaspoon of the filling on each circle. Follow the instructions for preparing the tortellini given on page 132, then place them on a large cloth and let dry for at least 3 or 4 hours.

Cook the tortellini in 8 quarts salted boiling water, to which oil has been added to prevent sticking. Stir gently with a wooden spoon. When the tortellini rise to the top of the pot, let them cook for 2 or 3 more minutes, then test for doneness. Remove with a large slotted spoon and place in a large serving bowl. Pour in the remaining 4 tablespoons butter (which you have melted). Toss gently, add the warmed cream, and the ½ cup cheese. Toss well and serve in soup bowls, adding a dash of pepper over each serving.

*Serves 6 to 8.*

One of the greatest pleasures of entertaining is to watch your dinner guests enjoying your efforts. It provides the incentive to constantly improve your cooking. One of the reasons we love having Fernando Lamas and his wife Esther Williams at our dinner parties is because they not only adore Italian food, but because their conversation is scintillating. However, you do have to give them lots of advance notice because they are usually quite busy.

I had a sudden urge to give a small dinner party one Saturday night, so I called Esther the day before. She said she didn't think they could make it because they had tickets to the opera but she would check with Fernando and let me know. She called me first thing Saturday morning and said, "Flora, Fernando said we're coming." I was really surprised because I knew they were big opera buffs. "What happened to the opera?" I asked. She told me Fernando said, "I can always get a recording of the opera, but I can't get a recording of Flora's pasta." That really pleased me. Oh, the power of a good dish of pasta!

That night we had Conchiglie con Ricotta and it was a pleasure for me to see Fernando enjoying it so much. He just kept coming back for more and more, and that, my friends, made all my efforts in the kitchen worthwhile.

—Flora

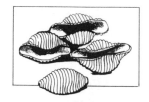

# 97. Conchiglie con Ricotta al Forno

## (Baked Shells with Ricotta)

3 Tbs. salt
18 to 24 giant shells
1 Tbs. olive oil

Filling:

1 lb. ricotta
1 tsp. chopped Italian parsley
1 egg, beaten
2 pinches ground nutmeg
  salt and freshly milled black pepper to taste
1 cup diced mozzarella cheese
3 Tbs. freshly grated parmigiano cheese

3 cups Bolognese sauce (page 12)
3 Tbs. freshly grated parmigiano cheese

Cook the shells in 7 to 8 quarts salted boiling water, to which you have added the oil to keep the shells from sticking. Cook until very *al dente*, about 10 minutes. Drain well, and let cook, keeping them separated. Place the ricotta, parsley, egg, nutmeg, and salt and pepper in a large bowl and mix well. Then fold in the mozzarella and the parmigiano and mix well.

Preheat oven to 400 degrees.

By this time, the shells should be cool enough to handle. Stuff the shells with the ricotta mixture. Place them in a buttered baking dish, side by side. Spoon a liberal amount of sauce over the shells. Bake for 15 minutes. Sprinkle with parmigiano and serve in soup bowls, 3 or 4 shells per portion. Bring remaining sauce to table.

*Serves 4 to 6.*

## 98.  Lasagne con Gamberi e Granchio

**(Lasagne with Shrimp and Crab Meat)**

¼  cup olive oil
½  medium yellow onion, chopped
1  clove garlic, minced
1  tsp. chopped fresh parsley
1  stalk celery, chopped
½  lb. crab meat, cooked and shredded
½  lb. medium shrimp, cooked, deveined, and cut
   into 2 or 3 pieces (you can find these in any
   good fish market)
1  cup marinara sauce (page 9)
½  cup dry sherry
   freshly milled black pepper to taste

1  lb. lasagne, packaged or homemade (page 5)
3  Tbs. salt
1  Tbs. oil

1  recipe béchamel sauce (page 13)

In a large skillet, heat the oil and sauté the onion, garlic, parsley, and celery until the onion is light golden. Add the crab meat and shrimp and let simmer over a low flame for 5 minutes, mixing well. Add the marinara sauce, sherry, and pepper, and stir well. Then cover and let simmer over a low flame for 10 minutes. Turn off the flame and let stand.

Cook the pasta in 5 to 6 quarts salted boiling water, to which oil has been added to prevent sticking. Cook until very *al dente*. Drain pasta and place it on a large cloth to dry.

Preheat oven to 400 degrees.

In a buttered baking dish, lay out a bottom layer of lasagne. Spoon over this some of the seafood sauce. Next, another layer of pasta, with some béchamel sauce spooned on. Then repeat: pasta, seafood sauce, pasta, béchamel sauce, until all the ingredients are used up, ending with the béchamel sauce on top. Bake for 15 minutes. Cut portions into squares and serve in flat dishes.

*Serves 4 to 6.*

This recipe comes from a very special place, the Self-Realization Fellowship center in Los Angeles. This society was founded by Paramahansa Yogananda in the United States in 1920, after he founded the Yogoda Satsanga Society of India in 1917. It is a worldwide organization with temples, ashrams, and meditation groups and centers throughout the United States and thirty-eight other countries.

The monks and nuns of the Order are vegetarians, and since they cook daily for the ashram residents, I felt sure they would have a pasta recipe. Many of the nuns of the Self-Realization Fellowship are friends of mine, so I telephoned the ashram and one of the nuns said, yes, they did have a lasagne recipe which was a big favorite there. She gave it to me and I am only too happy to include it in this book. As you can see, this recipe has proportions on a much larger scale than the other recipes, very handy for when one is giving a larger-than-usual dinner party.

I consider this recipe to be very special, particularly because it comes from the Self-Realization Fellowship in Los Angeles. My association with Paramahansa Yogananda's society has changed the lives of my family and me and we have never been happier. Roberto and Antony are also members—and I feel that this recipe carries with it a special blessing. My wish is that you, too, will benefit from this "spiritualized" dish—from its spiritual* as well as gustatory savor.

—Flora

* For those of you who might be interested in the spiritual side of what I have related here, I would suggest you read the book, *Autobiography of a Yogi* (Los Angeles: Self-Realization Fellowship, 1959), which is Paramahansa Yogananda's life story. Or you may contact Self-Realization Fellowship, 3880 San Rafael Avenue, Los Angeles, California 90065, for information about the yoga meditation teachings they offer.

## 99. Old-Style Lasagne

Sauce:

2 cups olive oil
8 cloves garlic, chopped

8 cups onions, chopped
2 qt. tomato paste
8 bay leaves
½ cup dried basil
¼ cup dried oregano
salt to taste
1 cup chopped fresh parsley
2 cans (6 lb. 6 oz.) tomatoes
1 gal. water
2 cups freshly grated parmigiano cheese

3 lb. lasagne
6 Tbs. salt

5 lb. mozzarella cheese, thinly sliced
4 lb. ricotta, thinly sliced
1 cup freshly grated parmigiano cheese

In a very large pot, heat the oil and sauté the garlic and onions until soft. Turn off the flame and let stand. Process the tomatoes in a food blender for 10 seconds at lowest speed. Now add to the sautéed onions in the large pot the bay leaves, basil, oregano, salt, parsley, tomatoes, tomato paste, and water. Mix well, then let simmer for 1½ hours. Add the 2 cups parmigiano just before turning off the flame, mixing in well.

To make the pasta, break the lasagne in half and cook in 5 quarts salted boiling water, to which you have added 1 tablespoon oil, until *al dente*. Stir to prevent sticking together. Drain and set to dry on a large cloth.

Preheat oven to 375 degrees.

Remove bay leaves and spoon a small amount of sauce on the bottom of a very large baking dish or two. Alternate with layers of lasagne, mozzarella, and ricotta, spooning some of the sauce over each layer. End with a layer of ricotta. Sprinkle the top with the 1 cup parmigiano cheese. Bake for 20 minutes.

*Serves 25.*

# Index